COLOR

COLOR
Natural Palettes for Painted Rooms

Donald Kaufman

and

Taffy Dahl

PHOTOGRAPHS BY TINA FREEMAN

TEXT BY LAUREL GRAEBER
COORDINATED BY SUZANNE BUTTERFIELD

DESIGN BY JOLENE CUYLER

CLARKSON POTTER/PUBLISHERS
NEW YORK

ACKNOWLEDGMENTS

This book is the result of an intensive collaboration with Suzanne Butterfield, who
was instrumental in the realization of every aspect. She helped formulate and focus the
basic ideas; organized approaches to publishing, photography, and writing; and labored in
the trenches for over three years to resolve the myriad details. Her diligence and professionalism
inspired the effort throughout. We are grateful that we were able to make the journey with her.
In addition, we wish to express appreciation to our clients and other color enthusiasts, who
not only allowed us to photograph their homes, but who also gave us help and encouragement.
We especially wish to thank Monica Barco, who organized the photography in Provence,
and helped us uncover these extraordinary color atmospheres of the Luberon.
Our great thanks go to Robert Isabell for providing flowers and for his inspiration.
And finally, we wish to express our appreciation to our editor, Carol Southern,
who saw the idea from the beginning and guided us precisely in its realization.

The authors were involved in creating colors and palettes for most but not all of the locations featured.

*The color swatches that accompany the photographs are meant to represent the actual paint palette used in the space. Color photography and
reproduction processes may cause them to vary slightly from the real paint colors.*

The painting on the bottom of page 11 is *Summer Day on Conesus Lake* by John Frederick Kensett. The Metropolitan
Museum of Art, bequest of Collis P. Huntington, 1900. (25.110.5)

The Mission House in Stockbridge, MA, property of The Trustees of Reservations, is open to the public on a seasonal
basis. It is featured on pages 136–143 and 156–161.

Copyright © 1992 by Donald Kaufman
Photographs copyright © 1992 by Tina Freeman

Published by Clarkson N. Potter, Inc., 201 East 50th Street, New York, New York 10022. Member of the Crown
Publishing Group.

CLARKSON POTTER, POTTER, and colophon are trademarks of Clarkson N. Potter, Inc.
Manufactured in Japan

Library of Congress Cataloging-in-Publication Data
Kaufman, Donald.
Color: natural palettes for painted rooms/Donald Kaufman and Taffy Dahl; photographs by Tina Freeman; text by
Laurel Graeber.
1. Color in interior decoration.   2. Interior walls.   I. Dahl, Taffy.   II. Graeber, Laurel.   III. Title.
728—dc20   NK2115.5.C6K38   1991   90-27244
ISBN 0-517-57660-0

3   5   7   9   10   8   6   4

FOREWORD

BY TIMOTHY FERRIS

Who would believe that so small a space could contain all the images of the universe?
—LEONARDO DA VINCI, ON THE EYE

More light!
—GOETHE'S LAST WORDS

OLOR CONSTITUTES ONE OF THE DEEPEST OF THE MANY mysteries that confront us when we investigate the relationship between the human brain and the wider world.

The physicists say that colors correspond to various frequencies of oscillation of an electromagnetic field: Red is low frequency, violet is high frequency, and yellow lies in between, at the center of the spectrum of light to which our eyes are sensitive. (This is not a coincidence. The sun is a yellow star, we evolved in sunlight, and so the range of colors we can see approximates that of the sunlight that reaches Earth's surface.)

The neurophysiologists, for their part, tell us that the color-sensitive cells of the eye employ only three pigments. This may account for the origin of the schoolbook doctrine that there are three "primary" colors, from which all others can be made; the primary colors are characteristic, not of the universe, but of the way we look at the universe. If so, the eye works rather like a television tube, which builds a range of hues by painting the TV screen with dots of only three colors—red, green, and blue—in differing intensities. Using this simple approach, the brain can distinguish an estimated seven *million* different colors.

But such insights, useful as they are, fall far short of explaining the miracle of vision. The eye is part of the brain. Like the rest of the brain, it engages in an active interrogation of the perceived world. The results may look unaffectedly realistic, and certainly they resemble reality—we wouldn't survive for long if they didn't—but in actuality they are highly selective.

For example, we see high-resolution images only at the center of our field of vision: the rest is low-resolution, presumably to improve the brain's data-processing speed. Yet we feel that we are seeing everything clearly, thanks to a pleasant fabrication put together in the brain. Similarly, few of us notice that we have a blind spot in each eye. (To find it, cover one eye, hold a dime at arm's length and slowly move it off toward one side; with a little practice you will find the spot where the dime disappears. An Enlightenment king of France employed this trick to "cut the heads off" offending ministers who bored him in cabinet meetings.) Nor are we normally aware that our eyes emphasize straight lines and edges over curves and fuzzy boundaries, or that they detect motion more readily in peripheral than direct vision.

The list of such idiosyncracies is long. My point is that the eye is an active agent, not a passive instrument like a camera. (Nor, for that matter, is a camera all that passive, so long as a human being is operating it; think of Ansel Adams, scrambling up mountain peaks, tinkering with lenses and emulsions and exposure times, dodging and burning his prints, all to concoct realistic-looking portraits of the outdoors.)

Small wonder that the ancient Greeks thought of vision as a beam shot outward from the eye. We *make* the world we see, and researchers trying to understand this subtle process have found it necessary to study not only the allegedly objective world in front of the eye, but also the subjective world behind it.

Artists as well as scientists have contributed to this effort. When Leonardo da Vinci wrote that colors seen in shadow become more alike as the shadows deepen, he was exploring the inner world of eye and brain. (The color-detecting cells in the retina are too insensitive to fire at low light levels, and consequently we see few colors at dusk, none by starlight.) Stare intently at a bright red apple and then look away, and you will see a green ghost apple. This phenomenon, which scientists today theorize is caused by temporary exhaustion of the pigments in the relevant photosensitive cells, was vividly described in the eighteenth century by the poet Goethe. "On one occasion I stopped at an inn toward evening," he writes, in his book *Theory of Color*. "Presently there entered an attractive young woman with a radiantly white face and black hair who wore a scarlet bodice. From a distance I looked at her intently in the dim twilight. When she left I saw on the white wall opposite me a black face surrounded by a bright glow; the apparel of the utterly distinct figure appeared in a beautiful sea green color."

Don Kaufman belongs to the tradition of artists who reflect on the nature of their work and its relationship to perception. When I first met him he was dressed in a house painter's white coveralls, standing atop a ladder, painting a ceiling in my fiancée's new home in Los Angeles. "Don is a painter," Carolyn told me then. I thought she was stating the obvious: There he was, after all, painting the ceiling. What I did not understand was that Don is a *painter*—an artist whose canvases are in the collections of the Whitney Museum, the Museum of Modern Art, and the Hirshhorn—and that he was now painting rooms and buildings because his works of art had kept growing larger, until he outgrew canvas and began coloring the whole world.

Today, Don works with his wife and partner Taffy Dahl, who left her career as a ceramic artist to collaborate. They are known as "colorists," a term that their work has served to both expand and intensify. People who have the privilege of living in homes they have painted remark on how their colors do not so much mimic the hues of nature as re-create their effect. Don and Taffy's colors look simple—they seldom assert themselves, and instead create fields of light within which almost any combination of people, furniture, books and paintings, and cats and dogs can settle down in admirable harmony. But in reality they are highly complex. They embody Leonardo's dictum that the color of any one object "partakes of the color of surrounding objects." What they borrow from nature is nature's habit of mixing many different colors with one another, so that each is distinct while none seems out of place.

It amuses me to consider how disconcerting Don and Taffy's working methods must be to clients who confuse creativity with mere virtuosity. Where a headstrong decorator might come barging in to a country villa, declaring that *here* there is to be a slab of cobalt blue, *there* a splash of orange, they are more often to be found down on one knee in the surrounding woods, picking up leaves and pebbles and scraps of tree bark and scrutinizing them for clues to nature's palette. Don and Taffy mix their colors slowly, for they are out to echo natural processes that take longer still, and the results can be as harmonious with their surroundings as an Incan hemp bridge or a Huron birch canoe. And that is true of all genuinely creative art; it works to reunite the realms before and behind the eye, to make the world whole.

This unique volume opens an aperture onto Don and Taffy's work, as faithfully as ink and printing press can reproduce it. Some will regard their work as art, which of course it is. I prefer to think of it as something new from nature.

T.F.
New York, 1991

CONTENTS

INTRODUCTION

PICTURE A ROOM WITH A BLUE CEILING, A GREEN CARPET, RED chairs, and yellow walls. The combination sounds strident, even unsettling. But now imagine opening a door and walking outside. Depending on the time of day, the season, and the weather, the sky may be blue or violet, the grass green or brown, and the surrounding foliage a variety of hues, deepening from green and yellow to russet and gold. The colors are the same in both scenarios. One sounds contrived and garish; the other, natural and beautiful. Yet, if the room could be given the nuance, the subtlety, the textural elements—and the light—of the outdoor scene, it could be beautiful as well.

The premise of this book is that elements of a space can, and should, be colored to create the same enriching and luminous atmosphere we experience in nature. A room realized in this way will have a feeling of completeness that embraces not only the relationships among surfaces and objects, but the character of the space itself. Giving it color will go beyond enhancing four walls to enhancing the empty air they surround. But real space is never empty. The ever-changing hues of the sky, from the roses and golds of dawn to the indigo of evening, demonstrate that the air is filled with particles ranging from drops of mist to motes of dust. Light does not just pass through them—it will be transmitted, reflected, or absorbed in varying degrees.

Through this process, the atmosphere itself takes on color.

Seen in these terms, color does not depend on its inherent qualities, but on circumstance. We may think of the sun as revealing the landscape's "true colors," but the colors at noon are no more true than the ones at dusk. In every second of observation, the interactions of light, surface, and human perception create the hues anew. And because sensitivity to color differs among individuals, each person's perception will be unique in some way, based on what he has just perceived and all that he has perceived before.

Thinking of color as a process may make it seem hard to

control. In fact, it can be as well orchestrated as a film shot under different light conditions. It is possible to know, for example, how the natural light streaming into a room is going to look at different times; it will seem whitest in bright daylight, most violet in shadow. Artificial illumination provides its own color for light—yellow, if it comes from an incandescent lamp. But the color of the source only partially influences the atmosphere. The character of the afternoon light in a room with a black marble floor will not be the same as it is in a room whose planks are bleached pine, even if the paint on the walls is identical. Every surface plays a role.

In nature, that role is rich indeed. Here, the subtleties of shape and texture create numerous gradations of color. The color of tree bark, for example, is a collection of numerous warm tones created by the bumpy journey of light across its rough-edged planes. Even a leaf is not simply green. The partial transparency of its surface allows it to transmit light as well as reflect it. This interplay of color and texture gives the natural world its endless variety—a variety not often seen in a painted wall.

Natural colors are also complex, meaning that they comprise many different hues. We may speak of a lime green or a robin's-egg blue, but if we examine the fruit or the egg, we'll see that the dominant color contains hints and echoes of other hues, both

warm and cool. These subtle differences are like visual reminders of the true source of color: light. Because sunlight is really the most colored of all—it contains red, yellow, orange, green, blue, and violet— any surface it strikes will reflect these hues in varying amounts. The resulting color is not an absolute, but a matter of degree. That is why nothing in nature is one pure hue, and why no two elements in its palette ever clash. Ultimately, the beauty of natural colors is that they produce a luminous atmosphere—seen together, they re-create the full spectrum of light.

Using color that has the same properties as natural light is far from a new idea; the principle has guided artists for centuries. Impressionist technique, for instance, is based

on using a full spectrum of hues to create thousands of points of simultaneous contrast that the eye interprets as light. In seventeenth-century landscapes and the paintings of the Hudson River Luminists, brushes of cool color on warm grounds yield the same luminous effects. And as in nature, these colors are always balanced across the spectrum. Look at a nineteenth-century seascape by J. M. W. Turner, and just a hint of red in a boat may provide all the necessary weight to balance the blues and greens of sea and sky. The aesthetic pleasure that results from looking at such a composition is not learned, but natural —the human eye easily tires of one color family; it actively seeks the complementary hue.

What do these observations mean for the rooms in which we live? An architectural space is like any other work of art —it has a cohesiveness that embraces everything from its boundaries to its smallest detail. For either a painting or a room, the atmosphere binds all other elements. In either case, the approach to color is the same: leave out nothing that nature includes.

For architectural spaces, this means employing the artist's approach—mixing each color with all the hues inherent in light. This has not been the standard practice of paint companies, whose color formulas usually consist of only two or three pigments. Any color, even gray, may be made up of a dozen or more hues. Instead of following the usual paint formula and adding black to the mix, a rich gray can be created by combining all of the primary colors. The result is a neutral whose composition ranges across the spectrum. Every other mix destined for the same space should be just as complex. The actual amounts of the pigments will vary with the requirements of the

space and its illumination, but every color in the palette should include some of every other color.

Such complex formulas not only enable a wide variety of hues to harmonize as they do in nature, but they establish an equation: full-spectrum colors equal light. The room's atmosphere becomes a dynamic process of colors interacting under different conditions. Even if the conditions themselves cannot be controlled, such as the available sunlight, they can be observed and then interpreted through color to realize the space as a luminous and beautiful whole.

The landscape offers many simple clues to achieving this spectral completion without garishness. The universally beautiful combination of sand and sea, for instance, involves the pairing of delicately nuanced colors from opposite ends of the spectrum—yellow and blue. Some might argue that this spectral opposition is a good reason not to combine them. In fact, it is the most important reason for putting them together. If you follow this subtle example, realizing the full potential may be only a matter of providing moldings that are a gentle shade of buttermilk to complement pale blue walls.

Complex colors also give painted walls the textural dimensions of natural surfaces, whose varying smoothness or roughness influences their ability to reflect light. The scattering of light by a large number of pigments in a paint film gives a surface the illusion of luminosity and depth, which is why a wall painted with a complex color can appear to be a subtle gradation rather than a monolithic plane.

Finally, the placement of color is as critical to the atmosphere as the hue's composition. Each color should somehow serve form, whether it is to enhance the architecture's existing shapes, or to disguise them in favor of new ones that color creates. This idea of a hierarchy of forms expressed by a complete spectrum applies not only to an individual space, but to the entire aggregate of spaces. Juxtapositions of warm and cool color, and the luminosity they create, should carry over not only from wall to wall, but room to room.

These principles still allow complete freedom in the selection of individual hues. No color is inherently wrong, although its particular amount, intensity, or depth may indeed be wrong for the light of a particular space. An overall palette can come from nothing more concrete than personal preference, but its specific composition will be a process of discovery, a search for the specific formulas that will create the richest atmosphere in that individual setting, whether it is seen at noon or midnight, by sun or by incandescent light, through a distant doorway or right at its threshold. By manipulating the variables that create color, any number of combinations can be achieved that will bring life and, literally, light to the architectural space.

CREATING THE ARCHITECTURE

Color can extend walls, raise ceilings, eliminate corners. Reaching beyond the limits of construction, it can sculpt a new space whose borders are defined purely by the spectrum, whose geometry consists not of carpenters' planes, but of the lines where one hue begins and another one ends. Walls may be fixed, but painted surfaces can appear to move. Unbound by the rules of conventional placement, color creates an architecture all its own.

VIVID SUNSET AT THE END OF A BLEAK DAY always astonishes. Even though its pinks, violets, and golds are inherent in the light we see, their revelation is like an unexpected gift: The ordinary becomes the beautiful.

This New York apartment of designer Alexander Julian delivers a similar surprise. Its colors appear to have been distilled from the twilight. Just as the sun's rays filtered through evening mist enable us to see the world with a new richness, these pigments transform blank, boxlike rooms into spaces that flow into and out of each other with easy grace.

This effect is based on natural phenomena. Although we may not be aware of it, every color we see outdoors is enhanced by the simultaneous presence of color from the other end of the spectrum. Rose would not be as beautiful in the evening sky without a touch of violet. The same principle applies to these rooms. Each has both warm and cool colors that play off of each other, encompassing the entire spectrum. The hues draw the eye from one color range to another, engendering a kind of movement, and achieving a completeness that we usually see only in nature.

While blues and violets predominate here, they are balanced by their complements of reds and yellows, expressed softly in tones of coral and buttermilk. These colors contrast, but they also harmonize. The juxtaposition of a coral frame and a lavender doorway gives each color more definition, yet they look no more garish together than an African violet in a clay pot.

Just as important as the range of colors is the way they are used. Because the apartment receives abundant sunlight, deep tones enrich the space without threatening to darken it at midday. And their placement defies the architecture: In one room, the paint on a single wall continues past the molding onto the ceiling, so that these surfaces create the effect of a canopy. In other areas, the walls and the ceiling are painted the same color. This technique helps to erase the boundary between them, much as the horizon, when seen from a boat's deck, seems to dissolve into the sea. The colors and their flat, low-gloss surface make the rooms appear to be atmospheres rather than accidents of geometry. The result is two homes within the same space: one is a fact of construction; the other, a creation of color.

THE PALETTE

Only strong colors could erase the boundaries between walls and ceilings of this urban apartment and remain vivid in the bright light. The interplay of blues and violets with corals and yellows constantly redefines the dimensions of the space.

The unconventional
placement of color changes
walled enclosures to
interactive planes.

PREVIOUS PAGE: *In the
dining room, the deep
lavender of one wall is
bordered by complementary
color—buttermilk on the
adjacent wall, coral on the
door trim.*

ABOVE: *The ceramic pillars
are by Constance Leslie.*
BELOW: *In a sunset, as
here, the intensity of each
hue softens the rest.*

RIGHT: *In the living
room, the steel blue of the
fireplace wall continues onto
the ceiling, negating their
boundaries.*

PREVIOUS SPREAD, LEFT: *A spectral range of color, just as bright as the apartment's, can be seen in wisteria blossoms tumbling across an old wall and door. There is green in the foliage, orange in the earth and bricks, violet in the flowers.*

PREVIOUS SPREAD, RIGHT: *Zolotone—a sprayed-on mixture of thirteen different pigments —looks almost like fabric on one wall of the living room.*

The lack of window treatments and the simplicity of the furnishings keep the decorative focus on color. Warm and cool hues frame each other, creating the impression of motion.

ABOVE: *The blues and violets of the living room open onto the mauve and yellow tones of the dining room. The painting is by Billy Al Bengston.*

*Another view of the same
doorway shows aquamarine
trim framing the colors on
one side, coral on the other.
The geometric furnishings
include an American late
1800s horn chair and a
1930s console.*

EVERY CITY SEEMS TO HAVE HIDDEN CITIES WITHIN it: the new forms created by the interplay of light and shadow when the sun strikes its buildings, or when nighttime illumination turns its skyscrapers into glittering needles. Although the architecture is the same, the cityscape changes from hour to hour.

In this urban apartment, color was used to mold a series of structures that a bland coat of paint could not have defined. Like figures emerging from the mist, various shapes now stand out and give the space scale and energy. Although all the colors are essentially neutral, their interaction creates the appearance of movement.

When deciding how to approach the two-story studio, the owner had to determine which areas of the space were most important. The ceiling, the window walls, and the core of the apartment—a cube that housed the kitchen within it and the sleeping loft on top of it—seemed to call for colors that were as central to the spectrum as their positions were to the architecture. Also potentially exciting was the tall stack on one side of the loft. When given color, it could create the illusion of continuing through the ceiling and into the sky. Finally, the largest volume of space, but perhaps the least distinguished, was the shell of the apartment. This included the wall behind the sleeping loft, where the studio's door was placed, and the side wall that served as a backdrop for a stairway descending into the living area. It also embraced an irregular and relatively uninteresting first-floor wall of closets adjacent to the sleeping loft.

With the spaces so ranked, the individual hues could be chosen. One color was a given: the bright yellow-orange of the wood-plank floor. As is usually the case, the rest of the palette derived from what the owner loved, ranging from the smoky blues and grays of his modern art to the soft buff tones of his dog's fur.

Because the central cube was the design focus, it received the warmest color—a soft butter shade. Darker neutrals frame it: a fog blue that covers the shell of the apartment and its staircase, and a violet gray that defines the soaring pillar on one side of the loft. A pale shade, almost like that of very bleached driftwood, coats the ceiling and window walls. Its warmth is a softer echo of the floor planks and the cube. Together, these subtle but still noticeable hues represent the full spectrum and transform the apartment into its own cityscape, one carved with color.

THE PALETTE

Because warm colors always draw the eye, the focal point of this apartment was given a golden tone; the secondary areas, smokier grays and blues. Although all are essentially light neutrals, their variation redefines the planes of the space. Some areas advance, others recede.

OPENING PAGE:
Contrasting colors make the basic geometric shapes of this apartment stand out in sculptural relief.
OPPOSITE: *The central cubelike mass was given a warm buttery shade, making it appear to advance. Framing it on the left is a pillar in pewter gray, and on the right, a wall in fog blue.*

ABOVE: *The stairs leading from the second-story entrance to the living areas blend in with the cool neutral tone of the south and west walls. Nearby is a 1950s leather chair and a 40s cast-iron flower stand.*
LEFT: *In this painting of Venice by J.M.W. Turner, a similar interplay of warm and cool tones emphasizes some structures, de-emphasizes others.*

ABOVE: *This painting by Luigi Campanelli helped inspire the palette. The bright plank floor and its 1950s carpet were also key, leading to the choice of a pale buff tone for the north and east walls and ceiling. The fifties furniture includes an Italian chair still covered in its original upholstery.*

RIGHT: *A view from the entrance highlights the pattern of cool neutrals framing warm ones. The ceiling and window walls provide a visual link to the strong wood of the floor; the rest of the perimeter is cool.*

WITH ITS STEAMY CLIMATE, abundant blossoms, and almost liquid sunlight, Louisiana evokes the tropics. Contemplating the color of these lush surroundings, architect Leonard Salvato decided to incorporate them into the classic lines of his New Orleans house. Although he created a contemporary add-on, color was as much his building tool as design. The deep ocher of the new kitchen wing and the green-blue of its adjacent tiles and pool create the illusion that the landscape has melted into the materials.

But although this palette reflects the ubiquitous polarities of hue in nature, it was art that inspired Salvato's choice. To make the different parts of the house harmonize, the architect used a full spectrum of color taken directly from the work of Impressionist and Post-Impressionist painters.

The new back wing, for instance, which cuts into the house like a wedge, seems to have leapt from the fiery palette of one of Gauguin's tropical landscapes. In fact, the architect borrowed the color directly from the artist's painting entitled *Contes Barbares*. In the painting, deep oranges and golds suffuse skin and hair. These ocher hues are balanced by the deep blues and greens of the sky and the foliage, and the violet of the man's robe.

The colors used inside and out depend on the same kinds of contrasts. Like the painting, they play off the most primitive of opposites: fire and water. Yet these reds and blues partake of each other in their composition, and together they span the spectrum—and they add up to light. The sheer brilliance of the Southern sun demanded these very intense hues, as did the construction. The deep ocher of the new wing helps unite the contemporary architecture with the surrounding earth, at the same time that the pale yellow of the house's old exterior mediates both the ocher add-on and the blues and greens of water and sky. Inside the house, more reds, blues, and yellows continue the pattern. The pale yellow tone of the hall and the light periwinkle and cream colors of the dining room are balanced by the warm rust of the kitchen on one side and the deep aquamarine of the living room. Not only walls intersect, but colors, creating visual bridges.

THE PALETTE

The colors in this New Orleans house were inspired by the warm reds and the cool blues and greens of a Gauguin painting. The dynamic placement of the hues distinguishes the original architecture from the contemporary add-on and provides another dimension to the house.

OPENING PAGE: *The fiery red addition cuts visually and structurally into the body of the house.*

OPPOSITE, TOP LEFT: *The source of the warm color is this 1902 painting,* Contes Barbares *by Gauguin.*

OPPOSITE, TOP RIGHT: *A combination of blues covers the glazed living room walls. One of Monet's water-lily paintings inspired the color.*

OPPOSITE, BOTTOM: *The more traditional dining room is painted with soft stripes, then glazed, creating a subtle shimmer. The adjoining rooms—the new red kitchen and the yellow hall—complement its coolness.*

LEFT: *In the living room, furnishings and accents repeat the glowing red.*

EXPRESSING THE ARCHITECTURE

Color can reinforce design, adding another layer of meaning to the parameters of a space. A different hue might define each architectural element, drawing attention to the overall structure. Or color may highlight just one grand detail, or details. It can guide the eyes through an entire building, showing how the rooms flow into and out of each other like the regions of the spectrum. Often, it is the language that translates the work of the architect into a rich vernacular.

THE ARCHITECT CHARLES GWATHMEY COMPARES this house to a cubist painting. Although its order may at first appear random, the geometry of the spaces unfolds in a definite series of patterns. It is not, however, a design that can be absorbed at one glance. Instead, the house reveals itself layer by layer through the related languages of architecture and color.

The exterior, for instance, is both the shell of the house and the source of its palette. Here, natural hues abound: the silvery beige of cedar shingles, the gray-green of Vermont slate, the red-orange of old brick pavers. These elements laid the groundwork for the design not only structurally, but visually. As the house developed with these materials, so did its colors.

First to be considered were the hues for the interior's perimeter. The ideal choice would create an interaction between the grid of the window frames and the adjoining surfaces. Through the use of a warm vanilla for the walls and a deep sage for the window trim—complementary shades—the perimeter gained a subtle shimmer.

Next in the hierarchy of shapes—and therefore in the hierarchy of colors— were two elements that refer directly to each other. The first is the fireplace. Because it is the focus of the two-story living room, it received the strongest pigmentation. Echoing the fireplace in shape and material is the stucco guest cottage across from the house. The architect saw them both as anchors for the design: the fireplace and its soaring stacks automatically catch the eye of anyone gazing in; the guest house draws the glance of anyone looking out. Both were defined by the same strong colors: warm terra cottas and deep blues at their borders, and ochers in between. In effect, each is a spectrum by itself. And while highly pigmented, they do not depart from the established color code of cedar, stucco, slate, and brick.

With these color families in residence, every other hue became their offspring. Whether the house is viewed from the center to its outer walls, or its outer walls to its center, each shade is either a derivative of warm reds and yellows or cool blues and greens. The interplay of these spectral opposites contributes to the house's energy. No placement is random; each choice sets up the next one. Every shape and color defines a specific part of a much larger whole, and echoes the rhythmic pattern of the architecture.

THE PALETTE

The building blocks of Vermont slate, brick pavers, and cedar shingles determined the colors. In each section, the hues travel from warm reds to steely blues, always mediated by yellows that vary from apricot to cream. The color layering follows the architecture.

OPENING PAGE: *A balcony view of the two-story living room shows the full palette as it progresses from level to level.*

LEFT: *This side of the living room reveals the color coding of its geometric shapes.*

ABOVE: *Vanilla and cream shades are complemented by sage green and slate blue.*

BELOW: *Each color was derived from one of the building elements.*

*The warmth of the house's
facade is repeated on the
interior walls; the cool colors
of the exterior trim
are echoed by the various
framing elements.*

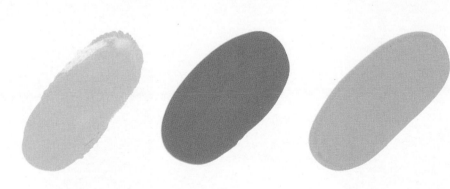

Changes in color represent variations in the design. The six-foot ceilings are a pale driftwood shade; the nine-foot ceilings are a deeper sand color.

The sequence of colors in the
house imitates the spectrum.
Varieties of yellow act as a
bridge between areas of
warm reds and steely blues.

The design of this bathroom echoes both the geometric grid of the windows and the gray-green slate and silvery beige shingles of the house's exterior.

ABOVE LEFT: *The view through these windows shows the stucco guest house, whose bright colors mimic the colors of the living room fireplace.*

ABOVE RIGHT: *The complex topography of these natural materials enriches their color, a phenomenon seen throughout the house.*

LEFT: *A variety of woods add to the warm reds and yellows of the rooms, complemented everywhere by the cooler trim.*

NOTHING SEEMS MORE APPROPRIATE FOR A seaside retreat than a gentle wash of color that evokes the luminosity of a summer morning. Each room of this house expresses this metaphor, from the dawn pastels that cover the walls to the earthy sisal flooring that recalls the garden.

But the palette for this cottage, decorated by Joseph D'Urso, did not derive solely from its airy environment on the shore of Long Island. Probably designed by a disciple of the architect Stanford White, the house is rich in structural detail. Flourishes such as columns, ceiling beams, and elaborate wainscoting give drama and definition to the interiors. Given these conditions—the brilliance of summer light and the abundant detail—it seemed natural to paint the moldings and wainscoting a balanced white, a color that would highlight the crisp architecture and not overwhelm it. The walls and ceilings needed to be dark enough to contrast with the white, but pale enough to be in harmony with the atmosphere. This meant that the intensity of each color was just as important as the hue.

Consider, for example, the first floor of the house. The custard tone applied to the central hallway can be regarded as a form of yellow—the central color of the spectrum used in the actual core of the house. This shade, however, does not draw the eye away from the stairway moldings or the latticework of doors and windows. Opening off the hall are rooms whose ceilings and walls are covered in pastels from other areas of the spectrum: a dining room in pale peach, usually a flattering color for entertaining, and a library in an icy blue that immediately evokes the first swim of the season. Everywhere, the white covering the architectural trim appears balanced, neither bluish nor golden—an ideal foil.

In areas of the house where architecture does not have a central role, color ceases to be a supporting player. In a small upstairs bedroom, for instance, a crown molding provides the only detail. In such an unadorned and limited space, color can be more intense. Here, a deeper gray-blue softens the room and echoes its atmosphere, which is smokier and less sunny than that of the downstairs spaces. Throughout the house, the accent pieces are also vivid flashes of color and texture that recall the brilliance of a few wildflowers in a vast meadow.

THE PALETTE

Without calling attention to itself, white sets off this summer house's architectural detail. The crisp, pastel wall tones contrast with the woodwork, but are still pale enough to be understated. Although recognizable as colors, they have the filmy quality of summer light.

OPENING PAGE: *A pair of century-old beech trees shade the house, designed in the Stanford White school.*
OPPOSITE, ABOVE LEFT: *The blue library opens off the hall, representing the cool side of the spectrum.*
OPPOSITE, ABOVE RIGHT: *In the living room, a soft gray color defines the ceiling coffers.*
OPPOSITE, LEFT: *In the entry hall, a pale custard tone marks the center of the house and the center of the spectrum. The soft peach dining room on the hall's other side subtly expresses warm color.*

ABOVE LEFT AND RIGHT: *The antique blue glass on the dining room mantelpiece contrasts with the rosy background.*
LEFT: *The same satin enamel white, neither golden nor bluish, was used for architectural detail everywhere. In the library, it highlights the elaborate moldings and decorative flourishes; pale blue walls give the room serenity.*

ABOVE: *In this yellow and white bedroom, the black floor silhouettes antique furnishings.*

OPPOSITE, TOP LEFT: *The simplicity of the space gives bright-colored pieces, such as this bentwood chair and hooked rug, a graphic appeal.*

OPPOSITE, TOP RIGHT: *Patches of color in an Ellsworth Kelly painting punctuate the quiet of the library.*

OPPOSITE, BOTTOM: *A crown molding was the only detail in this guest room, so a stronger color was chosen for the walls. It emphasizes the shadows, making the brass beds look adrift.*

LIMITING
COLOR

Color need not be noticeable to have a noticeable effect. All that is needed to create a luminous atmosphere is the interplay of warm and cool, sunshine and shadow. Two colors can be only subtly different, but still make a powerful duet. Even one hue can be made to play many roles. Sometimes texture itself produces enough visual variety to give the impression of a full spectrum of light.

A VARIETY OF WORLDS COEXIST IN THIS URBAN penthouse. Contemporary art enlivens the same space as nineteenth-century architectural drawings, and furniture in sweeping curves inhabits the same room as absolutely rectilinear designs. Works of different countries and periods mix, so that Art Deco French may sit side by side with 1950s American. Color's wide embrace binds them all, while still enabling each to stand alone. Just enough hue softens their neutral environment, enhancing the collection but not overpowering it.

The most pervasive color is that of the herringbone-patterned wood floor, which is stained almost ebony. Repeating like a refrain throughout the main rooms, it serves as a reminder that all color is relative to its context. Without this dark wood, the tints of the walls would be more perceptible. Because of its influence, the other colors function like white, even though they range from lavender to smoky peach to an extremely light aqua. They also flow naturally from their settings. The gray and ruddy shade of the dining room walls was taken from the reddish stone of the marble fireplace. The aqua of the garden room reflects both the paint on the steel shelves and the green of the planter boxes found just outside. In the living room, the palest of violets plays off both the 1920s French Aubusson carpet and the gray and black of the metal 1940s folding patio chairs.

Subtle as these colors are, they still influence the impression of the space. Because there is no difference between the wall and ceiling hue in either the living room or the dining room, each becomes its own world, a kind of cloud floating over a sea of black. Going from one room to the other entails not just crossing a threshold, but traveling from color to color. By accentuating the differences in the atmospheres of the rooms, this approach gives the entire apartment the illusion of more spaciousness and depth.

Where no neutral backgrounds are required for art, the color shifts become more dramatic. In the kitchen, electric blue trim and the limited use of Zolotone—a paint mix in which particles of colors are allowed to float—echo the blue laminate and stainless steel of the decor and help the room celebrate its own irregular shape. At the same time, the kitchen and the garden room seem even farther away from the dining room, because their cool colors oppose its warmth.

THE PALETTE

These colors are dark enough to create interest, but light enough to remain neutral. Because the black floor makes the hues seem pale, they can afford to be more intense, while still functioning as white. The colors' variety makes the space look larger.

OPENING PAGE: *The living room is painted a soft violet that is barely noticeable when juxtaposed with the ebony-stained floor and prominent artworks, including this painting by Sam Francis.*

LEFT: *Particles of pigment, predominantly pink and green, give the walls of this powder room literal sparkle. This type of paint mix is called Zolotone. An illusion of more space is created by its pattern.*

ABOVE: *Years of weather and wear have created a similar mottled effect on an ancient stucco wall.*

A smoky peach dining room opens onto an electric-blue kitchen. The contrast also creates a feeling of greater distance and separation between the two spaces.

The apartment's colors play
off of the furnishings and
art. In the dining room, the
wall color alludes to the red
and gray found in both
the marble fireplace and
the architectural drawings.

ABOVE: *An extremely pale violet covers both the ceiling and walls of the living room, softening the effect of the irregular-shaped beams and rectilinear furniture.*
OPPOSITE: *The warm green and cool stone of this Alaskan rock surface are echoed in the garden room.*

RIGHT: *The color of the garden room's ceiling and walls appears white, but is actually a much lighter version of the paint on the shelves. The use of green creates a natural connection between the room and the terrace outside it.*

OLOR CREATES THE LUMINOUS ATMOSPHERE OF these rooms, even though color seems hardly obvious. But there is one very strong hue here, easily overlooked. The deep amber of the floor is so integral to its identity as wood that the surface tends to be perceived as a structural rather than a decorative element. Yet the rich honey shade of the planks is a catalyst for the entire space, enabling it to serve as a warm but neutral stage for the owner's art work and possessions.

In the living room, for instance, the off-white paint of the walls reflects the floor, giving the room a soft, golden glow. This light bathes such objects as a painting of the Greek twins, Castor and Pollux, and a collection of Venetian glass, highlighting their shapes without competing with their colors. The presence of black in the decor also heightens the impression of the apartment as a grand, classic theater. The few black pieces make the off-white paint appear lighter and warmer still, while the off-white makes the black seem slightly cool. The black also provides a conclusion to the room's interplay of light and dark, warm and cool, so that the viewer has traveled from one end of the spectrum to the other without really noticing specific colors.

A similar dynamic takes place in the bedroom, where the walls are a slightly warm gray. Again, the bright floor influences the atmosphere of the room, making the wall color appear even grayer, and giving the space a silvery cast in relation to the living room's gold. Such contrasts, subtle as they are, provide all that is needed for a rich visual experience.

THE PALETTE

The key to the design of this apartment is the bright amber floor. It plays off the soft white and gentle gray of the rooms, making some surfaces appear golden and warm, others silvery and cool. This serene background highlights the material and lines of the objects.

Sunlight reflecting off the gilt edges of a mantel gives this corner of the bedroom a honeyed glow.
LEFT: *A statue in St. Germain en Laye, France, acquires different highlights from the sun streaming through leaves.*
PREVIOUS PAGE: *This living room wall functions as an illuminated backdrop for a painting by Carlo Maria Mariani.*

The reflected warmth of the floor makes the dining area look like an oasis. The neutral background also silhouettes furnishings and accents.
RIGHT: *In nature, too, simple stone surfaces take on golden and silver casts from the interactions of shape, texture, and light.*

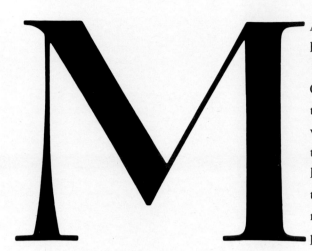

M ANY OLD HOUSES ARE REPUTED TO BE haunted, and at first glance, this early 1800s Creole cottage in the French Quarter of New Orleans would seem to be a grand example. The white walls frequently change color, sometimes shimmer, and even appear to release a silvery dew. These ethereal transformations, however, are due to natural, rather than supernatural, phenomena. The spell is being cast by the interactions of plaster, water, and light, not to mention the romantic imagination of the designers, Frank and Ann Masson, who wished to be as faithful to history as possible.

That meant forgoing a moisture barrier when the walls were replastered and stuccoed during a 1980s renovation. Instead, the walls were treated according to nineteenth-century standards. Two bricks thick, they were covered with a lime/sand mixture including a tiny amount of cement. Each of the three coats has a slightly different composition, and the last one is almost pure lime. A bit of umber powder was added to give the surface the beige cast it might have had 180 years ago, but the color is never consistent. The changing light and humidity, plus the variously sized granules of the coating, make the walls seem more fluid than solid. Water from the swampy ground seeps into them, leaving surface traces of mineral salts as it evaporates. These interactions give the walls a perpetually uneven surface, composed of materials that absorb and reflect light at different wavelengths so that the colors inevitably change.

Although the surfaces of this house could not yield data on the original colors, the designers, with an archaeologist, were able to determine the actual hues used in a similar period building. The result is a range of colors that captures all the haziness and warmth of the Gulf region.

One of the keys to the success of this palette is the calm of its environment. The simple, austere architecture does not detract from the softness of the walls, and little artificial light interferes with the slow shifts of the sun. (At night, the front parlor is illuminated only by candles.) The purity of the surroundings allows the colors to act out their own play, a historical romance that is no less stirring for its subtlety.

THE PALETTE

Many of the colors in this nineteenth-century house are created by texture rather than paint, as light travels across the rough plaster walls. The hues of the ceilings, stairs, and trim, mixed according to an archaeologist's analysis, evoke local soil, rock, and weathered wood.

OPENING PAGE: *Light reflected by a Flemish-style harpsichord bathes the parlor in a rosy glow.*
FAR LEFT: *The owners built a new staircase, using an archaeologist's report on another historic house to match the "greenish-gray" color of the risers.*
LEFT: *The changing surface of these flower petals and leaves creates the same variegated color as the old plaster.*

ABOVE: *A French nineteenth-century steel convent bed gives this atmosphere a touch of silver; the sun brings in gold.*
RIGHT: *Research for the colors centered on salvaged artifacts, including an old hinge and plaster chips.*
OPPOSITE: *The owners used historical techniques for the dining room fireplace, covering the plastered brick interior with a red-tinted, lime-based coating.*

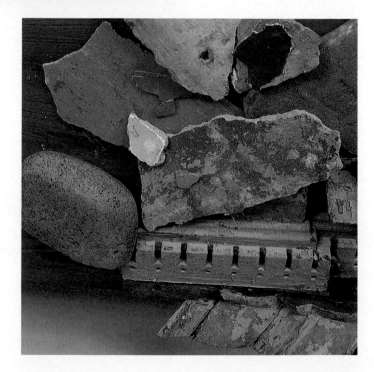

LEFT: *The speckled surface of an old brick walk and a panoply of leaves are other good examples of texture enriching hue.*

RIGHT: *Grays were used on both the exterior and interior trim. This view of the house shows the complementary effect of the blue-green doors and the ocher stuccoed walls intensified by natural light.*

NLY ONE COLOR IS TRULY ALL COLORS. It is white, the purity of light itself. Yet we rarely think of white as inherently rich, although we see its variety every day. Without white, we could never appreciate the shadowy blush of a rose, the golden haze of a cornfield, or the smoky blueness of mountains. We tend to regard such colors as constants, rather than creations of white light. But if we remember that light contains all of these colors, we can also understand how it can give each of them back.

This 1816 townhouse is all white, but never monochromatic. The paint is precisely the same mix from surface to surface and room to room, yet the light it reflects is always changing. The space that takes on a light blush at noon may seem slightly lavender in the twilight.

This subtle complexity is made possible only by combining many pigments. Like white light itself, the paint for these surfaces contains red, yellow, blue, and violet. If the proportion of one hue is slightly greater than the rest, it will give the white a certain cast. In this mix, the predominant violet makes the white seem ethereal. But the slight emphasis of one color over others is only part of the chemistry. The most important ingredient is the light itself. In each room, the amount constantly varies, so does the character of each surface, and so, inevitably, does the color. These shifts are gentle but very real. At midday, the plank floor makes the white appear softly yellow. The stairwell of brick, with its irregular surface casting luminous shadows, takes on the palest of violets.

Light, of course, is only partially within human control. We can open blinds or turn on a lamp, but we cannot make a room receive more sun. We can, however, control color. By observing the effect of light in a room over time and in space, we can deduce how color will respond to those changes. The process is like focusing a camera, seeking the point of greatest balance and clarity.

But why white? The use of one color everywhere allows its permutations to be a pure phenomenon of the walls' own texture and the rooms' natural light. And while any number of different colors could have been used, white seemed the ideal companion for the abundant sunshine that streams in.

THE PALETTE

A violet-tinged white composed of bright pigments was used for every painted surface, emphasizing the grand proportions of the space: but variations in texture and light make the rooms appear to have a variety of soft colors, ranging from pale gold in the sun to lavender at dusk.

OPENING PAGE: *The living room walls seem almost rosy in the sun, gray in shadow. The antique carved teak chairs are from the Philippines.*

LEFT: *Warm wood— pine planks and a birch Biedermeier sofa—add to the midday glow in this corner of the living room.*

ABOVE: *A white background emphasizes the shape and texture of objects, such as this hand-carved wooden seashell from Bali.*

Sunlight reflecting off the floor gives the dining room a subtle amber cast. The uniform color of the walls and ceiling allows the art and the furniture to be the focus; the painting by Alexander Vethers and French refectory table seem suspended in space.

The living room wall appears rosy and warm, the brick of the stairwell bluish and cool. Lighting and texture create the difference. The rough brick adds even more shadows to the dim hallway, while the smooth wall picks up warmth from the windows and surrounding wood.

OPPOSITE AND ABOVE: *Upstairs, even the floor is painted. The enveloping white gives the space the appearance of a sculpture garden—every object stands out.*
LEFT: *Other colors seem pure in such a neutral environment. The choice seemed particularly appropriate for the home of an artist, whose work area is shown here.*

LEFT: *Here, painted stairs have been allowed to wear, creating a romantic patina.* ABOVE: *In the living room, white silhouettes objects such as Meissen plates and American Empire footstools.* RIGHT: *The simple space is both understated and rich. This painting and all other art work shown is by Alexander Vethers.*

ABOVE: *Seashells are vivid examples of whites with different tones. This collection spans the entire spectrum, from rose to blue to violet.*
RIGHT: *In the master bedroom, the interplay of yellow light and blue shadows constantly varies the wall color.*

A T FIRST GLANCE, THE COLOR IN EACH OF these rooms appears to be the same on every surface. But although these neutral tones hardly vary in lightness or darkness, they do differ subtly in temperature. While one wall may resemble the palest yellow warmth of sunlight striking sand, another may express the cool crystal blue of frosted glass. And just as different surfaces within a room may be perceived as warm or cool, so can the entire room when compared to the one next to it. Yet seeing it at a different time of day or approaching it from a different direction can alter the impression completely, almost as if the colors had been shuffled.

The similarity of the hues actually creates the illusion that they have changed places. Because they differ so little, the slightest shift in illumination or perspective can bring out the cool side of a color that lately appeared warm, or the warm side of a color that lately appeared cool. In each space, the color of the floor has the greatest influence over these perceptions. The gray tones used in the library, for instance, seem to have a subtle blush when viewed against the steely gray of the carpet. But when seen from the living room, which has a light marble floor and a touch of gold in the palette, the library appears cooler, bluer, more stately. Similar transitions create a sense of movement from the garden room to the dining room. The stucco walls of the garden room appear cool next to the even warmer clay of the paved floor, and warm when viewed against the cooler charcoal color lining the archways. The charcoal is so cool that the pleated amber silk of the dining room ceiling, seen through the doorway, appears even warmer.

The elements of each room also stand out because the gradations in color reveal different aspects of the work of the architect, John Burgee. Prominent details are painted in warmer tones, creating the illusion of forward movement; backgrounds are cooler, making them appear to recede. A violet cast and a certain angle of viewing can enhance the depth of a painted panel or a shelf; an ivory cast can make a molding or a surface detail stand out in greater relief. What is almost never noticed is the color itself—it becomes a silent medium expressing the nuances of the design.

THE PALETTE

This apartment is filled with light neutrals, either slightly warm or slightly cool. Though the differences are subtle, any shift in perspective can create a different impression of the colors. Through their minute variation, they quietly underscore shifts in the architecture.

OPENING PAGE: *Seen beyond the cool shadows of the living room doorway, the library's gray palette looks warmer.*

LEFT: *When the living room is viewed from the library, it seems the warmer room because of its polished marble floor and sunlight.*

RIGHT: *A Mali headdress marks the door from the conservatory into the tented dining room. The charcoal trim of the archways makes each room look warm when approached from the other.*

BELOW: *Slight variations in warm and cool color define an Alaskan horizon.*

BELOW RIGHT: *The apartment's palette also expresses the architecture— relief surfaces are painted lighter than recessed ones.*

COMBINING INTENSITIES

Any observer of a field of wildflowers or a tropical rain forest is likely to be impressed not by the colors, but the color. The most riotous range of hues and the most vivid tones do not draw attention to themselves individually when all are equally bright. And if, as in nature, such colors represent a full spectrum, the effect will not be busy, but balanced. No color can be conspicuous by its absence—or presence— when every hue is proportionally displayed. Here are interiors where abandon is truly moderation.

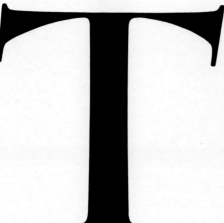

THE FAMILY THAT OWNS THIS PAIR OF COUNTRY houses is passionate about collecting—and passionate about color. These twin obsessions dominate the decor of both houses, which seem to have as many hues as they do objects. Nothing, however, seems excessive. The multitude of color and collectibles creates an atmosphere that is vivid overall, instead of one in which a single hue appears jarring by contrast.

This paradox is one of the keys to a satisfying use of color. Ordinarily, a very intense hue is best applied sparingly. But when a lot of strong color is a given, as it was in this family's array of porcelain, glass, and antique furniture, the backgrounds needed to be just as bold.

In both houses, a hall links the downstairs rooms. In the main house (pictured on page 102) this was the only area needing new color, since most of the other rooms were papered. Painting the hall white would have provided too stark a contrast with the furnishings, whereas a very deep color would have been overpowering in so large a space. The yellow glaze falls between these two extremes.

To enter the hall is to appreciate just what it means to be surrounded by a full range of color. The yellow hall represents the center of the spectrum, while the rooms that open off of it—a blue-papered living room and a library with rosy tones—express either end. Other design elements, such as the red stair runner, provide another mediating link between the warm and cool extremities of the spectrum. Because all hues are present, no single piece stands out.

In the farmhouse, yellow again became the heart of the design—this time, through the hall's traditional wallpaper. Blue and green were used with white in the dining room. The rest of the house demanded red. The salmon of the living room is an emphatic conclusion to the statement made by the other colors, and the even deeper red of the studio can only be seen as its exclamation point. This studio, a two-story addition, manages to be far more than just a red room—it is like a velvet casing for the collection. This shade, too, is a complex color, with a blue-red glaze covering a yellow-red undercoat.

The only hue not used in abundance here is green—and with reason. Verdant leaves and shadows are a gift from every window.

THE PALETTE

The bright hues and rich woods of this family's antiques called for strong colors in both houses pictured. Because deep color is found everywhere, no single element is overpowering and the use of a full spectrum gives the entire space a sense of completion.

PREVIOUS PAGE: *In the farmhouse, a rustic wood mantel and antique wallpaper frame a variety of objects.*

ABOVE: *The blue-green interior of a corner cupboard emphasizes its depth.*

RIGHT: *Colors shift from blue and green to red on this Italian stucco wall. The red walls of the studio also have complex layers—a blue-red glaze over a yellow-red background.*

OPPOSITE: *This two-story studio is like a jewel box, with deep red walls and ceiling setting off the bright blue and white of the porcelain collection.*

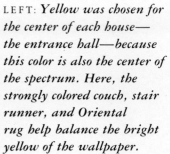

LEFT: *The white dining room wall emphasizes the deep colors of the glass collection in the window. Their gemlike quality immediately draws the eye.*

BELOW: *In the living room, a salmon tone was preferred over a peach. Its blue overtones harmonize with the cranberry-colored sofa and indigo rug, and provide a crisper contrast with the amber wood floors and yellow hall.*

A full spectrum of color is subtly at work in each room and throughout each floor. Here, the antique wallpaper of the dining room is blue-green with warm highlights. Just outside the door, the yellow hall makes a natural bridge to the salmon living room, which has cool overtones and accents.

The tone of the living
room appears rosier in this
corner, which has yellow
furnishings and abundant
light. Because the color has
both a warm and cool side,
it adapts easily to its
surroundings. The deep blue
of the Delft fireplace tiles
completes the spectrum.

A winding staircase
dominates the front hall of
the main house. The walls
are glazed, giving the
surface a slight textural
pattern that softens the
brilliant color. The yellow
was made bright enough
not to look brown in evening
light, but pale enough to
serve as a background for
art. The wall and ceiling
trim have been painted
with a slightly beige cast;
pure white would have
looked blue next to yellow.

LEFT: *The long weathering of this brick wall gives it many color nuances. Although it is also a strong yellow, the rough surface allows it to meld with its surroundings. The greenery and blue stone are its natural complements.*

BELOW: *The glaze on the hall walls makes them appear more luminous and transparent. The color is continued through a narrower passage that opens off the entryway. The low ceilings—sometimes only seven feet—are painted white to be unobtrusive against the intense hues of the walls.*

RIGHT: *The interiors are orchestrated so that anyone can perceive a full range of color from one room to another. In the aquamarine wallpapered living room, both the yellow hall and the red stair runner are visible. This complete spectrum of hues helps the multi-colored collections to blend together, with no object overshadowing the rest.*

LEFT: *Architectural elements such as pediments and moldings function as frames for the strongly colored spaces. Wood is also part of the palette, varying in color from soft chestnut to deepest mahogany.*

BELOW: *The pale ceiling and carpet of the living room balance the deep colors of wallpaper and furnishings. The many wood pieces occupy the red-orange end of the spectrum, adding warmth and rounding out the blues and yellows.*

RIGHT: *The bright yellow that runs through the heart of the house is itself a complex color. Although composed primarily of cadmium yellow, it contains an infinitesimal amount of rose madder and of cobalt blue.*

W HEN USING COLOR, SOME-
times more is actually less. If
a homeowner loves primary
hues, it is possible to use
them with abandon if no one
color stands out at the ex-
pense of the rest. In these
rooms designed by Garrett
Cane, for instance, yellow
covers the widest expanse,
but the equally intense red re-
fuses to be ignored. It marks the passage from one area of strong color to
another. With yellow and red selected, the next logical choice was brilliant
blue. The eye demanded it as a relief from the dominant warm colors; the
space demanded it because only a cool color could complete the spectrum.

Just as the choice of one color helped determine the rest, the placement of
each governed what could go next to it. Since placing two dissimilar colors
side by side heightens their contrast, a red would make an adjacent yellow
appear green. The decision to use both colors here meant that the yellow had
to have a rich, almost marmalade tone. Without that hint of orange in the
paint, the result would have looked sallow. Instead, the color appears pleas-
antly golden next to the red, while the blue furnishings and accents provide
the necessary cool counterpoint.

All of these effects are created through an understanding of the way color
is perceived. When the eye focuses on an intense hue, the color appears
gradually more gray. This happens as the eye's sensitivity to the intense shade
lessens, and it begins to seek and to register more of that color's complement
—the hue whose position on the spectrum is directly opposite. If the complementary color is present in the room, the visual
experience achieves its own equilibrium.

It is also easier to look at colors whose intensities are similar. Just as it is difficult to discern
subtle images in dim light immediately after you
have been in bright sunshine, it is hard to focus
on dull colors if you have been viewing very
bright ones. When this variable is eliminated,
the space maintains consistency and remains easier on the eye.

Because the intensities are balanced, this
apartment has steadiness as well as strength. Un-
abashedly vivid, it is as irresistible as a bright
new box of crayons.

THE PALETTE

**Strong colors can create
a balanced environment
if they are of the same
intensity and from
opposite parts of the
spectrum. In this
apartment, bold yellow
and red are countered
by brilliant blue. The
combination is actually
more restful than
one bright strong color.**

OPENING PAGE: *A chair made by the owners' son punctuates a bedroom wall.*
OPPOSITE: *Yellow envelops the living room. Its complement, blue, appears in decorative accents.*
ABOVE: *Because the eye interprets yellow as a light source, this kitchen appears to glow even in subdued light.*
LEFT: *The boldness of the hues echoes the drama of the objects, such as this mounted Indian stone torso.*

ABOVE: *Placing colors side by side heightens their contrast. The spaces' predominant yellow was given an orange cast so that it would not appear green when placed next to red.*
RIGHT: *Nature doesn't shy away from primaries, as seen in the deep yellow of this sunflower. Here, too, there is cool color in the blossom's center.*

OPPOSITE: *Red walls with mounted African masks mark a literal and visual passage from one area of the apartment to another.*

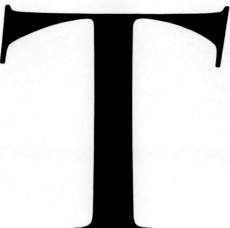

THE LATE BARBARA WOODHOUSE WROTE A BOOK in the early 1980s called *No Bad Dogs,* whose radical premise was that there was no such thing as a canine character inherently undesirable or irremediable. The same can be said of color. Although we may shy away from living with hues like chartreuse and tomato red, our distaste comes more from principle than practice. Who has ever tried them?

Here is a house that has. The Herman Grima mansion, a nineteenth-century bastion of Old New Orleans, is filled with such seemingly unwholesome associations as citron green and attar of roses, mustard yellow and ruby red. Yet these colors conform to both nature and history. They easily appear side by side in a garden, and frequently in restored houses. The Victorians, who were less afraid of passion when it involved decorating, often used strong hues, and sometimes the more bilious, the better.

The harmony of these colors derives from their very intensity—the brilliance of one prevents the brilliance of the next from becoming overwhelming. In one bedroom, for instance, the yellow walls might dominate the room, if it weren't for the deep red ball fringe of the canopy. Neither color can be completely arresting, as the gaze is always drawn somewhere else.

The various elements of the palette also function as complements, which guarantees their compatibility. Yellow, for instance, can be found in the ocher ceiling of the verandah, and blue in its slate-colored doors. These same hues exist in the buttery plaster of the walls and the gray-blue stone of the floor. Using deeper versions of this natural palette enriches the space with no risk of garishness. It brings design closer to nature, and nature closer to design.

THE PALETTE

More than a dozen intense colors work together in this historic New Orleans house. Ranging from yellow ocher to ruby red and citron green, each one moderates the effect of the others. Because these hues are complements, even extreme versions harmonize—a principle the Victorians often applied.

OPENING PAGE: *The citron green of the bed canopy balances the warmth of the walls, painted a historic color known as attar of roses.*
LEFT: *The bright contrast of this bed's ball fringe helps control and soften the strong yellow background.*
BELOW: *The sitting room includes a range of light and dark earth colors that emphasize the architecture.*
RIGHT: *On the porch, the ocher ceiling and blue doors reinforce the natural complements of the warm wood panels and stone floor.*

ENHANCING LIMITED LIGHT

Color can give dim rooms the rich glow of an ember or the comforting warmth of a loden coat. Instead of competing with the shadows, it can dissolve them with its own gentle fire. Deep, warm colors do this with their inherent luminosity. Adjusting their intensity to the level of light assures an atmosphere in which the boundaries of the room seem to seep into the air.

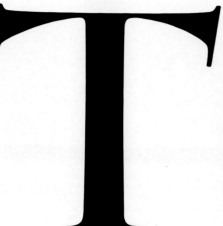

THE SOFT, GOLDEN LIGHT SUFFUSING THESE rooms seems to emanate from the walls rather than shine through the windows. A New York duplex with limited sun and lackluster views, this apartment had originally been painted in pale colors that only accentuated its shadows. With a new, deeper palette, the main rooms have acquired an amber glow that seems almost palpable—a visitor brushing against one of the walls half expects a dusting of cinnamon to fall on his shoulder.

This welcoming aura shows how much can be done with a lot of color and little light. The rich shades create an air of candlelit mystery particularly appropriate in a nineteenth-century building. Instead of attempting to attain the impossible—a sunny apartment—the color choices celebrate the ambiance of the rooms, turning their lack of light into an asset.

The magic of this color is its inherent warmth. Because shadow can tinge almost any hue with violet, these rooms could have easily looked mournful and cold. The space needed strong color from the other end of the spectrum. Because yellow pigment lacked the necessary depth, red became the palette's center. The paint for the living room was made to appear luminous with the use of a transparent red pigment. An abundance of gold and glass, including mirrors, hurricane lamps, and framed photographs, enhances the light further by continually reflecting it. The overall ruddy glow seems to color the air more than any one surface.

Adding warmth, however, does not mean sacrificing the quiet refreshment of cool color. In this room, all anyone need do for respite is look up—the blue ceiling floats overhead like a patch of clear sky. The balancing effect keeps the eye and the spirit from tiring. A similar dynamic is at work in the entry hall, where gray walls with a pink cast abut gray trim with a violet cast. Still other contrasts appear in the library's juxtaposition of warm wood paneling with a cooler white ceiling, and in the kitchen's pairing of cherry cabinetry with greenish marble. Although pure reds, greens, and blues may never be apparent in any of these surfaces, their pigments and materials still express those areas of the spectrum. Just as the living room's gray cornice appears warm against the blue ceiling and cool against the cinnamon walls, so each color, however subtle, inevitably relieves and renews those adjacent to it.

THE PALETTE

In this apartment, intense color takes the place of sunlight. The warmth comes from earthy shades balanced by cooler complements. The hues are adjusted to blend with the low level of light. Although highly colored, the space remains neutral.

OPENING PAGE: *The gray of the master bedroom contains red and violet. It is dark but not cold.*

LEFT: *The rich cinnamon color of the living room walls warms the space; the blue ceiling expands it.*

RIGHT: *The living room's glass and gilt objects add to the reflected glow.*

BELOW: *Similar color juxtapositions occur naturally. Gardens abound in deep, warm hues relieved by cool greens and blues.*

BELOW RIGHT: *The living room moldings and trim are painted in a neutral shade that looks cool adjacent to the walls, warm next to the ceiling.*

ABOVE: *In the kitchen, the colors come mainly from the materials—bright cherry wood and green-black marble. A soothing light gray paint covers the walls.*
RIGHT: *The entry hall's violet-gray trim frames the pink-gray of its walls and ceiling. The warm color echoes the carpet and subdues the irregular beams.*

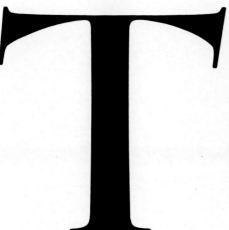

THE COLOR FOR THIS APARTMENT WAS DE-signed by the seat of the pants—literally. The owner, trying to describe his favorite color, found a perfect example in a rumpled pair of khaki trousers. But the dominant hue does more here than reflect personal taste: It is a perfect neutral to lend warmth to a dim living space, and an ideal starting point for a palette that enhances the available light.

Khaki a neutral? And appropriate for a dark environment? Although we think of khaki as a kind of green, this mix contains equivalent amounts of red, yellow, and blue, which enable it to harmonize with a variety of objects. And despite the lack of light, the khaki is also deep enough to be perceived as a color. Its very depth improves the space by eliminating the high contrast between pale walls and a shadowy interior. This color adapts to the low light; a pastel would announce it.

With any color, warmth is far more important than brightness or darkness in compensating for limited sun. These rooms gain luminosity through the colors' inherent glow rather than mere reflection of light. Even the cool shades in the palette have been mixed with oranges and yellows, which insure vibrancy in otherwise understated hues.

This embrace of deep color, however, doesn't mean that there is no use for pale tones in a dim space. In these rooms, at least one surface is dramatically lighter than the rest. In the living room, the ceiling is a pale cerulean that fulfills three functions. It maximizes reflection of the available light, it balances the warm khaki with a touch of coolness, and it helps articulate the other architectural features: ceiling beams and trim that are defined in other unobtrusive but distinct colors. The dining room and bedroom (not shown) reverse the pattern: Here, the ceilings are a deep shade while the walls are flattering tones of peach. In each case, the uses of the room influenced the choice of color and value. A deep blush on the dining room ceiling bathes the occupants in a rosy glow. In the bedroom, where the ceiling is just as often a focal point as the walls, a deep terra-cotta lends drama. Only one color was selected for its reflective qualities alone: the cream covering the window sashes and muntins throughout. This versatile shade helps bring in light without violating the quintessential softness of the space.

THE PALETTE

These colors were designed to appear warm —even the cool tones have a trace of orange or yellow. At the same time, the khakis, browns, and reds are intense enough to be seen as colors in the dim space. To reflect available light, the trim and at least one surface are pale in each room.

PREVIOUS PAGE: *The khaki living room walls add warmth, while the paler ceilings and moldings add a brighter, cooler contrast.*
ABOVE: *The level of color is adjusted to the level of light. In the living room, the strong shade of the walls colors the shadows without attempting to erase them. The deep and earthy tone of objects, such as a yellow towle jardiniere and an iron garden gate, also dictated a darker background.*
RIGHT: *The light blue of the ceiling, framed by even paler moldings, keeps the wall color in check. The window sashes are a light cream to make the most of the incoming light.*

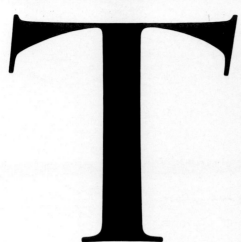HESE ROOMS ARE NOT FLOODED WITH SUN-
shine, and yet they have a light of their own.
The richness of the abundant wood and the
green walls create the feeling of sunlight flick-
ering through a canopy of leaves. Like a forest
in the afternoon, the space seems luminous
rather than lighted.

This golden atmosphere is largely the gift of
green. The one color that is simultaneously
warm and cool, green can create the illusion of
light without contrasting too sharply with the
space's intrinsic shadows. Whereas white walls would make the furniture and
beams appear darker, the equally intense green brings out the wood's warmth.
The cool, blue aspect of the color brightens the framework at the same time
that its warm, yellow side adds the subtle suggestion of sun. Because our eyes
are conditioned to seek light, a visitor's glance will be drawn naturally to the
luminosity this palette creates.

Details within the rooms, designed by the M (Group), also amplify their
warmth. The deep reds, yellows, and greens of the carpet and upholstery
fabrics and the many gold-framed prints contribute both to the apartment's
honey-drenched atmosphere and its immediate sense of comfort.

THE PALETTE

**Green can be both warm and cool. Its yellow side suggests light; its blue
side, shadow. It is an effective contrast for a variety of warm and cool
colors. In this apartment, it brightens the space at the same time that it
relieves and complements the red in the wood furnishings.**

PREVIOUS PAGE: *The wood of the wall panels, picture frames, and furniture has an inherent glow. The green background suggests even more warmth because of its yellow content.*
ABOVE: *Bright accents and flowers keep the emphasis on warmth.*
RIGHT: *The pale mats of the artworks help amplify the light.*
FAR RIGHT: *The interplay of green and its complement, red, is continued in the draperies and upholstery.*

WORKING
WITH
STRONG TRIM

The most vivid hues in a house are sometimes those of its own materials. The deep reds and yellows of the wood are givens even before the interior palette has been decided. In these cases, strong color can give each room a life of its own that is contained but not canceled by the woodwork. Like paintings, colors look best when they are not overwhelmed by their frames.

E ACH WALL OF THE MISSION HOUSE IS FRAMED LIKE A painting—a painting that evokes the eighteenth century. Built in Stockbridge, Massachusetts, in 1739 for John Sergeant, a young minister, the house served as both a home for Sergeant and his family and a place of worship for the local population. (The exterior is pictured on pages 156–161.) Pine, plentiful during the period, etches the planes of each room, appearing not only in moldings and paneling, but in corner posts. When the house was moved and restored in the late 1920s, the plaster walls bordered by the pine framework were treated like canvases, painted with the true colors of the past.

Though strong, these colors evoke dignity and serenity. The pine woodwork that physically confines them tempers their visual impact, giving each room both a separate identity and a structural link to the rest of the house. Because the hues are of equal intensity everywhere, they turn the richly colored spaces into a balanced composition.

Adherence to historical painting techniques further softens and unifies the colors. The paints, mixed as they would have been in the eighteenth century, contain egg tempera or buttermilk, which was popular as a base because it was believed to make paint resistant to weathering and difficult to remove. Also true to the period, the preparations were colored with materials straight from the New England environment. Ocher and brick dust, for example, create the blush in the master bedroom, while egg yolk imparts the golden hue seen in the parlor, halls, and kitchen. Such unusual ingredients as fireplace soot and Paris Green—a 1700s potato pesticide that was probably used decoratively after it lost its potency—provide the pigments for still other age-old formulas. Applied with rags and sponges to the rough plaster, these colors appear variegated and translucent rather than flat and opaque. The irregularity of the surfaces and the inherent unevenness of the naturally pigmented coatings contribute to this effect by scattering the light, creating broad expanses of color that seem almost to shimmer. Because both the paint and the surface are mottled, the color looks as if it is glowing from inside the thick plaster walls. Interestingly, the deep values of the hues only enhance this visual effect. Dark tones that might have seemed austere and oppressive on absolutely flat, smooth surfaces appear to have filtered into the air like candlelight through stained glass.

THE PALETTE

The paints in this eighteenth-century house were mixed using materials of the period. They contain buttermilk and egg tempera, colored by such traditionally used natural agents as brick dust and ashes. The interaction of light and pigment varies the range of color.

PREVIOUS PAGE: *The yellow upstairs hallway opens onto a bedroom in vivid green.*
ABOVE: *The pine trim and corner beams give the strong colors an equally strong frame.*

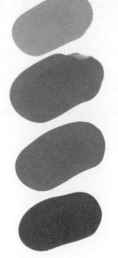

OPPOSITE, TOP: *The surfaces of leaves and rock naturally vary the quality of light. The dappled effect is also seen in the house.*
OPPOSITE, BOTTOM LEFT: *The palette downstairs mimics the spectrum—cool and warm rooms on either side of a yellow hall.*
OPPOSITE, BOTTOM RIGHT: *Egg yolks give the kitchen paint its brilliant color, while the mottled surface controls its intensity.*

ABOVE: *This conch shell in the front hall was used to call worshipers to church.*
LEFT: *Yellow paint, applied with rags to the rough plaster, creates gradations of color on the parlor walls.*
RIGHT: *The gray of the children's upstairs bedroom was achieved with a wash of buttermilk, eggs, and soot.*

OPPOSITE: *The traditional woodwork of the house visually unifies the individually colored spaces.* LEFT: *Cézanne used a full spectrum of hues to depict light hitting stone. The layering of red, blue, and yellow gives this painting,* Near the Pool at the Jas de Bouffan, *its rich and luminous quality.* BELOW LEFT: *This bedroom wall seems to glow from within, as the surface reflects and transmits light.* BELOW RIGHT: *The reddish brown of the beams provides a natural complement for the green of the back door.*

WHEN THE INTERIOR DE-signer Kevin Walz and his family acquired this weekend getaway, they didn't want to change its eccentric architecture, and couldn't change its dim ambient light. Decorating the space meant working within the strong boundaries the Victorian house already provided: a crazy-quilt geometry of wood beams and trim that gave the rooms a deep palette of chestnut and honey, golds and rusts. This bright and linear woodwork was like a frame that had been given to an artist even before he had had time to plan his landscape. The resulting picture would have to have at least as much character, or risk disappearing into its borders.

Even before the hues were chosen, it was clear that the rooms would have to be highly pigmented, since only a perceptible level of color could stand up to the intensity of the wood. The mottled surfaces of these moldings and frames, left with their original varnish, created multiple variations of orange and gold, which would further change the appearance of the adjacent walls. The light reflecting off oak beams or pine planks gave each space a tint, which varied with the position of the wood and the time of day. Painting the rooms' surfaces in deep colors would enhance the changes already present in the interplay of wood and light. Because there would be more color to react to the light, there would also be more dramatic shifts.

For use in an environment where so much color is perceived as red or gold, many of the paints selected came from the complementary green and violet areas of the spectrum. Because they balance the wood's strong color, they never overwhelm the rooms. These deep neutrals evoke slate rather than oyster or pearl, but when seen in context, they are almost unidentifiable. Acting in concert with the blush of the wood and the white of the light, they create a feeling of luminosity rather than the appearance of a specific hue.

The strength of these particular neutrals also allows the family to display furniture and art without having it appear overly silhouetted. Theirs is an especially eclectic mix, where, Kevin Walz fondly says, "the junk looks like art and the art looks like junk."

THE PALETTE
———

This Victorian house came with its own set of colors—light striking the abundant woodwork created bright oranges and yellows. The complementary neutrals selected for the interior emphasize lilac and green overtones. The paint and the wood temper each other.

PREVIOUS PAGE: *The cool neutral color of the living room walls receives warm overtones from the sunlight reflecting off the floor.*
ABOVE: *The gray dining room appears golden on one surface, dusty rose on another. Kevin Walz designed the stained Masonite and steel dining table. The pine sculpture is by Paul Bowen.*

LEFT: *The vestibule outside the dining room is a pale, warm violet. The light heightens the contrast of the spaces.*

BELOW LEFT: *The wood of an antique cupboard adds a green element to the color mix.*

BELOW RIGHT: *This freshly plowed field highlights the natural interactions of green, orange, and violet.*

ABOVE: *In the master bedroom, a violet-tinged gray subdues the strong wood elements.*

ABOVE RIGHT: *The intensity of the woodwork is like that of this weed silhouetted in a field of lavender.*

RIGHT: *The furnishings and accents continue the warm and cool themes. This wood "surfboard" table in the foyer is from The Red Studio.*

ABOVE: *The strong colors enhance the family's collectibles, but do not allow them to become obtrusive. Their eclectic mix of antiques and quirky found objects is a good match for the space.*

The bedrooms' deep colors accentuate the daily changes in the light.

LEFT: *In this little girl's room, the reflected light from a blue chair and weathered cupboard bring out the coolness of the mocha-shaded neutral walls.*

ABOVE: *A lilac shade in the guest bedroom is warmed and made more yellow by the afternoon sun.*

RIGHT: *In another bedroom, the warm- and cool-toned accents amplify the shifts of light and shadow across the nutmeg-colored walls.*

RIGHT AND BELOW
RIGHT: *These Lloyd loom
dining chairs combine the
primary colors.*
BELOW LEFT: *The eccentric
architecture of the house
includes Victorian detailing
and four enclosed porches.*

LEFT: *A colorful mosaic of handmade tiles shows how the surface variation enriches color.*

ABOVE: *A bathroom changes dramatically with the light. With natural illumination, left, the upper half of the wall develops just a suggestion of gold; with an incandescent bulb, it gets a more obvious dose of yellow and pink.*

INTEGRATING NATURE

Nature is the ultimate source of every palette. When asked to describe a color, we use terms like moss green, indigo blue, saffron yellow, cherry red. It seems impossible to imagine the hue without thinking of something in nature that expresses its character. The color seems almost to be the soul of that plant, that flower, that stone. This quality of natural color, which appears to be more in the surface than on it, can be imitated through design.

REATING COMPLEX FORMULAS IS ONLY HALF the task of imitating color in nature. The pebbly facade of a stone wall, the veil of moss hanging from a cypress tree, the brindling of bark on a branch all contribute to subtle variations in hue. These surfaces appear lively not only because their irregular facets reflect light in a variety of ways, but because they partially transmit it.

This building, the Mission House in Stockbridge, Massachusetts, shows how such color can be taken from nature and made to blend with it. Built over 250 years ago, the house seems as rooted in the soil as the New England rock that marks the tombs in the churchyard. It does not appear to be painted gray—it *is* gray. The oneness of the edifice with its environment comes from its mimicry of natural gradations of color. Although the exterior is all one hue, it is covered with a stain that allows the grain of the wood to show through. As light penetrates the grain, it gives the surface the illusion of depth. The interplay of light and texture causes the color to appear cool in some angles, warm in others. As sunlight and shadow shift across the facade, the color seems sometimes violet, sometimes periwinkle, sometimes slate. It is a treatment that allows a color to show every side of itself.

THE PALETTE

The gray that covers this eighteenth-century house is as complex and varied as the color of bark or aged New England rock. It represents essentially a middle range of all the grays of the landscape. The wood's rough character changes the hue continually, while the porosity of the surface gives it depth.

Memento Mori

N Memory of Mr Josia
son of Mr Josiah Jones o
...on he Died March
...1769 in y 69th year
...his Age

OPENING PAGE: *The stain of the facade softens the surface and emphasizes the effects of time.*

PREVIOUS SPREAD: *Age and weather have given the house and this tombstone similar coloring, ranging from cinnamon to cerulean.*

OPPOSITE TOP: *The textural variations of moss and lichen create patches of warm and cool tones.*

OPPOSITE BOTTOM: *Natural color includes many gradations, as seen in this churchyard.*

ABOVE: *Radiance comes from light bouncing off irregular surfaces.*

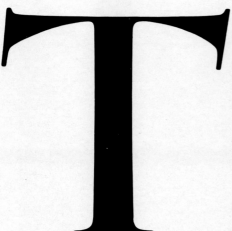

THE QUEST FOR BEAUTIFUL COLORS MAY BEGIN and end at the doorstep of the house. This was literally true for Maison Curiale, a historic house perched above a valley of ocher mines in Southern France. Renovated by the architect Christophe Huet, the former stone ruin displays a palette that was culled from the landscape. The surrounding volcanic rock yielded the brilliant blues, the terra-cotta stones lent the variety of reds, and the ocher that runs through the earth like a hidden trough of sunshine provided the range of yellows. Every one of these colors appears inside with the same infinite variety that it assumes in nature. Instead of being built there, the house seems to have sprung from the earth.

Although many of these hues were inherent in the building materials, they were reformulated before they were applied. For instance, particles of multicolored sand, washed out when ocher is purified, were added back in before the pigment was used. And because even the hand of the craftsman makes a difference in how color is perceived, the shade is never quite the same from one wall to another, or even within one small area. These manmade variations, combined with the naturally rough and ever-changing textures of stones, tile, and sand, create a kind of echo chamber for light, which bounces off the surfaces in an infinite number of rusts and yellows.

The richness of the colors also comes from their relationship to one another. Blue, the complement to the earth's ocher tones and burnt siennas, appears on the kitchen counters and the window shutters. It mimics exactly the deep shade of the nearby hill. White, traditionally perceived as the absence of color, makes a wall of this house seem to float forward from its darker surroundings. And while nothing may appear to be green, the juxtaposition of colors within the space —such as the yellow-white of 2,000-year-old lime covering a wall of red bricks—creates it naturally. Yet no one sees this wall as red, yellow, and green, any more than he sees the sun as a globe that has been colored red and orange. The color has achieved what it always does in nature: It seems to be not just on the surface, but within it. The walls and floors are not pastel versions of the materials of the region—they are their natural colors. The simple architecture is in keeping with its surroundings and expresses its strong, elemental quality.

THE PALETTE

This house of old stone is above a valley of ocher mines, whose natural red and yellow pigments appear in different mixes throughout the space. Cool complements—deep blues and greens—evoke the sky and hills of Provence. All the colors are rendered full strength as in the landscape.

PREVIOUS PAGE: *At the entrance, the naturally red wall, yellow door frame, and blue stones create a full spectrum. The seventeenth-century marker is from an old pillar; the height of the archway reflects the period, when few people were taller than five-and-one-half feet.*
LEFT: *In an abandoned factory nearby, the walls of the old stone rooms used to store ocher are impregnated with the pigment. Light plays across the irregular particles and rough surfaces, continually enriching the color.*

RIGHT: *Yellow ocher and violet-blue volcanic rock illustrate the polarities of the local palette.*
FAR RIGHT: *Particles of multicolored sand mixed with the ocher amplify the changes in light along the walls. Here, in the dining area, an old tailor's table and a tiled bench and floor contribute different reds to the color mix; an old wheelbarrow complements them with gray-blues and greens.*

LEFT: *The blue of the shutters is a signature color for this region of France, identical to the tone of the hills and sky.*

ABOVE: *A view of the terrace shows how each color of the house has its counterpart in the landscape.*

RIGHT: *The ocher of these walls is naturally deep, a striking complement to the azure sky. Red doors and a blue bench repeat the pattern.*

ABOVE: *Next to an ancient fountain is a cedar door from Afghanistan. The survivor of an eighteenth-century fire, it has many textural and color nuances.*
LEFT: *The yellow ocher deposits and their many striations yield hues from mustard-green to pale gold.*

LEFT: *The white wall of the kitchen is covered with 2,000-year-old lime, mixed with white sand and a trace of yellow pigment. The contrast of the yellow-green lime and the red bricks beneath creates a luminous effect. On the counter, the cobalt blue tile is a counter-point to the warm wood and stone. Benches taken from the Paris Metro are a humorous urban touch.*

BELOW: *The rosy tones of the workroom derive from red ocher and lime walls and a tile floor. The door was painted on each side to match the walls.*

LEFT: *One of the original ocher factories shows where the pigment was refined. The wooden and metal framework and the ocher itself play off each other, creating a complex palette.*
ABOVE: *The exterior of a neighboring house bridges the spectrum with green, orange, and violet—which are the same hues seen in the foliage.*
RIGHT: *Even a rusted metal door in the village has as many gradations in color as the adjacent stone wall.*

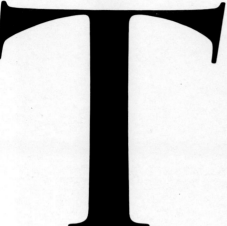

THIS HOUSE IS NEW, BUT ITS PALETTE IS TIME-less. The colors come from its building elements, which derive from nature itself. There is no red here that cannot be found in the dusty rose of mottled brick, no yellow that is not inherent in the warmth of raw or bleached oak, no gray that does not somehow echo the stone of the surrounding Berkshire Mountains. Even the one hue that stands out from its environment—the deep blue green of the front door—looks like an amplification of the sky and hills, the same chord rendered more deeply. The purity of the color and the spareness of the interiors create an austere beauty that is artless and ageless, unmistakably New England.

The simplicity of these colors, however, does not diminish their impact. Specific hues rarely declare themselves, and yet the house contains an entire spectrum that mimics nature in its diversity. Like the bark of the surrounding trees, the exterior trim and siding of the house do not appear to be one gray or blue, but many. The golden sheen that hovers like a cloud in the rooms does not come from one type of yellow, but from the many ochers and ambers contained in the unsealed plaster of the walls and ceilings, the knotted oak of the raw beams. The cool tones of the trim and the warm shades of the wood and brick frame a universe of color that only seems subtle because it is so natural. The earthy but often bright hues meld completely with the materials, allowing the house to appear colorful but not decorated.

Texture, one of nature's great color enhancers, was an important ingredient in the design. The brick of the floors has been brushed with unwashed bank sand, white cement, and lime; that of the fireplace with cement tinted with instant coffee. The variations in these surfaces and that of the plaster reflect light in myriad ways, giving these colors the same gradations observed in the landscape. The red oak floor, bleached and then stained with an oil tinted by white, ocher, and violet, attains a natural wood hue. On the exterior, the cedar roof and stained siding blend with the stone and trees.

Selecting the palette directly from the landscape precluded many of the laborious choices inherent in the design of a new house. Yet this simple answer was also the most complex one, giving the atmosphere a variety and richness that only nature itself can imitate.

THE PALETTE

The old stone walls and forests of the Berkshire Mountains contain the same range of neutral colors found in this summer house. Pigmented plaster, buttermilk-painted trim, bleached oak tinted with artist's oils, and masonry washed with cement and sand all enhance the hues.

OPENING PAGE: *Bleached oak floors and pigmented plaster give the interiors a natural warmth. The hand-crafted Windsor chair is by Peter Murkett.*

LEFT: *The walls' minute gradations in color come from their hand-troweled plaster surface.*

ABOVE: *The dining room, like the rest of the house, is framed with heavy unfinished oak beams. Their natural color is balanced by the cool gray paint on the architectural trim.*

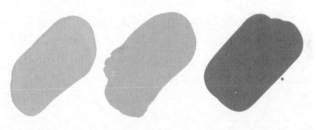

RIGHT: *The doors are covered with a deeper gray-blue milk paint, a complement to the yellow plaster and red brick.*
BELOW LEFT: *The golds, grays, and blue-greens of the New England countryside are repeated everywhere in the house.*
BELOW RIGHT: *The bricks of the living room fireplace are covered with cement tinted with an unusual pigment—instant coffee.*

ABOVE: *The bricks for the flooring, taken from an old courthouse, were brushed with cement made with riverbank sand. Some stone walls were also salvaged from the house, destroyed by fire, that originally stood on the site.*

ABOVE: *The stained siding and weathered cedar shingles imitate the subtle textural and color variations of the local trees and stone. The trim, slightly lighter and grayer than the other colors, frames the house.*

TOP LEFT: *The deep blue-green of the front door is the only strong accent, a punctuation mark for the facade.*

TOP RIGHT: *The interior doors and stair banister were painted with milk paint, and then finished with butcher's wax. The balusters are hand-shaved oak saplings.*

BOTTOM LEFT: *The bleached oak planks were stained with tinted oil for a natural, golden look, a counterpoint to the stony gray furnishings.*

BOTTOM RIGHT: *The complex shadings and highlights of rough bark and rock were imitated in the palette.*

EW SIGHTS APPEAR MORE UNIFORM IN HUE THAN A sandy dune or a field of wheat. In fact, few colors are more varied. Although these seem to fall within a narrow range of buffs and yellows, they actually span the entire spectrum from its coolest, most silvery side to its warmest, most golden glow. The constant variation in shape and texture of grains of sand or sheaves of wheat assures an abundance of color shifts.

This house in Provence is an object lesson in how such a simple vocabulary creates a poetry of its own. Every surface of the building, which was designed by Christophe Huet, either derives its color directly from a natural material or imitates one. The result is a careful blending in which it is difficult to tell what is nature and what is artifice, what is new and what is old. The house, built on a site containing a farm's stone walls and a threshing floor, seems to have grown and extended from these architectural roots. New floors of polished concrete, for example, have been colored to match the lime and sand found between the bricks of the ancient walls incorporated into the house. Where exterior wood abuts old stone, it has been tinted so that one seems to flow from the other. Plaster has been brushed with water and a yellow pigment to echo the subtle striations of age. A new interior wall, finished with cement before plastering, melds so well with the rough rock outdoors that a glass window seems less like a barrier than a veil strung across a passage of stone. When the concrete was poured for the wall, the architect filled the form with stones, which left irregular impressions that appear to have been made by the passage of time.

Yet there is also a certain modernity to the house, which was influenced by Japanese design as well as that of Greece and Provence. Simple geometric shapes, such as columns and cubes, stand out in the midst of its minimalist interiors. On the first floor, a wall of Plexiglas around the bathroom, covered by a wood grid, looks like an enormous Japanese lantern when illuminated at night. The whole style is sculptural, economically achieved.

Each of the building materials—and even every particle within each one—sounds an individual chord when struck by light. This varies the tone from space to space and hour to hour. And the different textures give the whole composition not only variety, but depth. What seem to be the palest of colors can create a rich atmosphere with a range of light and shadow.

THE PALETTE

Sand, stone, lime, and wood have lent their own colors to this house in Provence. Built on the site of an old threshing floor, the house draws a full spectrum of hues from nature. Even the few paint colors mimic the building materials, whose layers of texture enliven the palette.

PREVIOUS PAGE: *The stone walls of an old farm were incorporated into the house.*

ABOVE: *The spare interiors include both Greek and Oriental influences.*

RIGHT: *The bathroom's design highlights texture. Old stone and marble tile frame the porcelain tub.*

FAR RIGHT: *When illuminated, the Plexiglas wall behind the stairs looks like a Japanese lantern.*

ABOVE: *The existing exterior walls were braced and added to during the renovation. Any new concrete was tinted to match the lime and sand of the original walls. The stone paving outside was the threshing floor of the old farm.*

ABOVE: *To re-create the patterns and texture of age, stones were set into the form for this poured concrete wall.*

LEFT: *The palette of the house evokes the nearby wheat fields, where light constantly varies the color.*

DERIVING NEUTRALS

A neutral does not have to be a shade of white, beige, or gray. It need appear neither pale nor colorless. What it does require is a balance of warm and cool tones so that it can, in context, function as a color from either end of the spectrum. It will often be as deep or light as the objects it surrounds. Like a good understudy, a neutral can always take over any role.

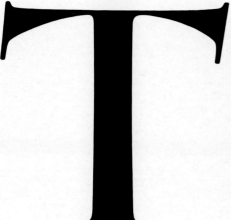

THE COLORS FOR THIS APARTMENT, A GRAND sweep of rooms overlooking Manhattan's East River, are essentially a reinvention of the palette of Jean Patellerie, an artist whose painting hangs prominently in the living room. The cool jades and warm bronzes of his canvas appear throughout the space, demonstrating that intense hues, whether created naturally or by an artist's brush, can function well as neutrals.

What makes these colors neutral is their context: strong, clean architecture and a variety of collections, ranging from 1930s pottery to antique needlepoint. In each room, the color is carefully calibrated to highlight both the dimensions of the space and the art within it. In a sense, the environment itself becomes a sculpture, because the color is applied not to emphasize the disparate elements of the architecture, but to reassemble them visually as a cohesive whole. The joined spaces look as if they had been carved from one solid mass.

For instance, a great wash of color, reminiscent of wet sand, covers almost all the surfaces of the living room and dining room. This unity of color turns two rooms, already connected spatially, into one majestic corridor. At the same time, the depth of the color assures that it will enhance the art. A paler shade would create too much of a contrast between the objects and their surroundings, making the scale of the rooms overwhelming. With this approach, the individual works become more integrated and the huge space itself gains a feeling of intimacy. Its geometry—that of a rectangle—asserts itself more when it is not broken up by different-colored planes.

When the color does shift, it does so dramatically. The wall of the hallway opening off of these rooms is celadon, a complementary cool tone that opens the space by making the wall appear to recede. The color of the library, a much smaller room, approaches earth in its darkness. Yet all of these colors are neutrals in their particular settings. They occupy the center of the scale between warm and cool, and they are tuned to the same pitch as the furnishings, the art, and the available light that surround them. A more subdued palette would have brought discord to this carefully balanced composition. Instead of a backdrop that draws the eye away from the objects, the rich color appears interwoven with the collection. The hues look almost as if they had been swept from the paintings onto the walls.

THE PALETTE

The warm sands and sea greens in this Manhattan penthouse were taken directly from the owner's art collection. The main colors were applied to unify the proportions of the rooms. Pale hues would have contrasted too much with the art, so these backgrounds are neutral but deep.

PREVIOUS PAGE: *The soft sand color of the dining room contains both warm and cool tones.*

ABOVE: *This neutral shade covers the walls and ceilings of the living room, providing a seamless backdrop for art.*

RIGHT: *A view of the water shows atmospheric warmth opposed by sea green—the theme of this design.*

FAR RIGHT: *This painting by Jean Patellerie and pottery by Jean Mayodon inspired the palette of these rooms.*

LEFT: *The master bedroom is in a misty neutral both warm and violet.*
RIGHT: *Sea green makes this bedroom a cool contrast to the rest of the apartment.*
BELOW LEFT: *A dark celadon hallway opens off the dining room. The color contrast enhances the distance between the spaces.*
BELOW RIGHT: *The use of a single color on walls and ceilings unifies the grand scale of the rooms.*

PICTURE A CROSSROADS WHERE EUROPEAN ELEGANCE meets the Wild West. While the furniture in these rooms includes a Venetian striped sofa, Victorian slipper chairs, and a Louis XVI chaise, the decor also boasts an antelope-patterned carpet, cactus drawings, and a stuffed armadillo. Shifting from deep sand to pale adobe, the neutral colors of the palette complement both the strength of this lively collection and the character of the light, a golden haze that filters through two front windows framed by flowing gray-green silk damask draperies.

The woman who lives in this New York apartment has her own name for the most extensive hue: Paris beige. Derived from the lining of the curtains, it is deep enough to provide a neutral backdrop for her gilded pieces and weighty chairs, yet light enough to be subtly atmospheric when used throughout the two main rooms. In effect, it is a balancing act: Its low intensity allows it to be relatively unobtrusive in the vast space, while its distinct color makes it a strong foil for the rich upholstery and eclectic woods and a subtle echo of the gold and bronze accents. Believing strongly that Manhattan apartments should not be made to look like country houses, this collector also sees it as a quintessentially "city shade," bespeaking both the urban and the urbane. At the same time, this color can be as reminiscent of the desert as the Continent.

Lighter hues border the main color. A buttermilk tone covers the walls of the entry hall between the living and dining rooms, then continues onto the imposing Federal moldings throughout. The contrast of the color and its repetition allow the spaces to appear framed yet still flowing. Another creamy shade articulates the crown molding, and the lightest covers the ceilings, where it can best reflect the midday sun and candlelight, the sole illumination in the evening.

At the other end of the apartment, a strong chintz dominates the bedroom. Because the owner didn't want the room overwhelmed by the pink fabric, the walls were given a clay color with strong apricot overtones. The paint tones down the fabric's assertive pattern and helps it harmonize with such unlikely design partners as rodeo posters and mounted springbok horns. The woman believes that the tones complement everything, even the fur of her cat. "The colors," she maintains, "are so full-spectrum that they set off everything that is put against them."

THE PALETTE

A soft beige, evoking the haziness of a Paris afternoon, harmonizes with the twilight atmosphere of this New York apartment. This dominant color is set off by lighter ones on the ceilings and Federal moldings. In the bedroom, where sun streams in, the hue brightens.

OPENING PAGE: *The warm shade of the living room walls echoes the many gilt accents, such as this Adam mirror.*

LEFT: *The color is balanced to embrace a wide variety of strong decoration, from Louis XVI furniture to an antelope-patterned carpet.*

ABOVE: *The bedroom's hue helps absorb the vividly patterned chintz and cancel out some of its pinkness.*

RIGHT: *The palette of the front rooms pivots around the neutral tone of the gray-green draperies.*

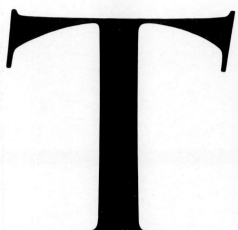

T HE MOST DISTINCTIVE COLORS IN THIS APART-ment are not the ones painted on the ceilings and walls. These surface hues, however, are absolutely critical to the perception of the colors that *are* important: those of the owner's art. Yet because this is a home and not an art gallery, the background colors had to provide warmth and an invitation not just to look, but to stay.

The tones that create this atmosphere were discovered in the unpainted canvas of a Morris Louis painting. Each of these colors was formulated not only to enhance any and all of the art works—which are sometimes moved from place to place—but to suit the specific requirements of the light, function, and size of each room. So although the subtle range of pinks, beiges, and creams may seem to vary only slightly from one area to the next, that minimal shift makes all the difference.

The foyer, for instance, is the smallest space, with the least natural light. The incandescent bulbs that usually illuminate it already give the area a large measure of yellow. This meant adopting a color with a trace of pink that would allow the space to seem warm in the low light of day, but not too warm when the lights were on in the evening.

Because the living room is larger, has ample light, and contains so much art, it needed a more formal and less decorative treatment. Its paint also has a touch of pink but is more gray or beige in its overall tone.

Far warmer is the dining room, whose paint has the most golden cast of all the colors in this family. It's a shade that remains within the palette but best expresses the convivial function of the room.

The most earthy hue is in the library, dominated by oak paneling. Only a green-shaded beige ocher would harmonize with these elements and preserve a neutral shell.

In all of these rooms, the placement of the colors reinforced their neutrality. Covering the ceiling and walls with the same paint eliminated any hint of contrast that might draw the eye away from the paintings. The juxtaposition of the hues with the deep wood floors also insured an impression of a more or less white background. But a subtle cream paint covering the moldings highlights the boundaries of each room and the differences between them—differences that depend not on transitions from warm to cool hues, or light to dark, but on changes in intensity.

THE PALETTE

The warm cast of bare canvas sets the tone for this apartment. The paints were mixed to be as golden as possible but still neutral enough to serve as backdrops for art. Within this range, each room is individually colored according to its light and dimensions.

OPENING PAGE: *The warmth of the living room walls surrounds the cool blue of a Miró canvas.*
LEFT: *The living room's ceiling and walls have the most neutral tone, making the art the focus. The painting next to the early nineteenth-century chair is by Clyfford Still. Visible through the alcove is the dining room, with a painting by Kenneth Noland.*
RIGHT: *The range of tones in this Paul Klee painting echoes that of the apartment.*

ABOVE: *The foyer opens onto the living room, left, and the dining room, right. The latter's color is slightly warmer for intimacy.*

TOP LEFT: *The master bedroom includes a mirror-back chair, designed by Anne Beetz from a 1927 Mies van der Rohe sketch.*
TOP RIGHT: *The bedroom walls have the least color, and blend with the carpet for a restful effect.*

BOTTOM LEFT: *The unprimed canvas in the large Morris Louis painting in the living room was the genesis for the palette.*
BOTTOM RIGHT: *A Calder mobile marks the entry to*

the library. The room's oak paneling and floor dictated more green in the wall color.

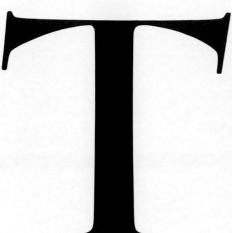

TO CROSS THE THRESHOLD OF THIS MEDIEVAL house is not to leave the world of nature, but to re-enter it. In the entry hall, a thick bed of river stones crushes softly beneath the visitor's feet, while the massive walls display the subtle effects of wind and weather. This is a house in which raw, mottled rock shares its complex palette everywhere, natural wood asserts itself through deliberately weathered paint, and even an occasional hollyhock waves from between the stone pavers. The blue of a shutter or door seems to have been rubbed like chalk off the nearby mountain, while the soft hues of plastered walls were created from sand dredged from the nearby riverbeds. Called "La Louve" for the last of the wolves inhabiting the countryside, the house seems to have absorbed the wild spirit of its name.

The real orchestrator of this beauty is designer Nicole de Vésian, who has planned her surroundings with art rather than artifice. Believing no colors can compete with those of nature, she has mixed the sand from three different rivers as if they were oils she had squeezed onto a palette. The results are neutral colors that express the basic polarities of nature: One shade for the wall plaster is predominantly blue-green, the other yellow-red. They reflect the same differences we see between winter light and summer light, between the glow of the moon and the fire of the sun, between the silvery velvet nap observed on the underside of a garden leaf and its warmer, more golden-green surface. This color variety, which inevitably develops outdoors, has been brought inside simply by allowing natural materials to be themselves. They extend from the simple straw of baskets and sisal floor coverings to the plain canvas that Ms. de Vésian has hung around the windows with shower hooks.

The result is a house that captures all the change and impermanence of nature itself. Never the same on a June morning as they are on a December afternoon, these are neutrals that not only have two sides, but four seasons.

Ironically, the human touch behind La Louve's design is most evident in the garden, where the furniture was painted to dissolve into the landscape and an ancient well was turned into a pool. The owner has also introduced her own geometry, clipping the trees and shrubs into her favorite shape—a sphere. It's where nature imitates art in a kind of whimsical reassertion of order.

THE PALETTE

Almost nothing in this setting is artificial. Sand from the banks of three different rivers colored the plaster. The exterior and interior colors are from the same families, but cooler outdoors, warmer within. All painted surfaces imitate the many hues of the surrounding landscape.

PREVIOUS PAGE: *A bed of river stones covers the floor of the entry.*

ABOVE: *A humorous touch in the living room is a broken faïence plate whose halves are glued above and below one of the shelves.*

RIGHT: *Color comes from natural materials such as leather, sisal, weathered wood, and plain canvas, which is hung on shower hooks as curtains.*

FAR RIGHT: *Riverbed sand in three tones was used to tint the plaster coating for the stone walls. The living room is a warm yellow-red shade.*

OPPOSITE: *The plastered stone of the entry appears golden in direct sunlight, a silvery brown in shadow.*
ABOVE: *An herb garden surrounds the ancient well, which has been made into a pool. The variety of color in the stones and foliage is repeated in the house.*
LEFT: *Like cool rock against warm earth, the gray-blue shutters complement the sandy exterior walls.*

ABOVE: *The "summer living room" opens onto the garden through three large bay windows. The furniture is the same color as the shutters, a stony blue counterpoint to the warm sisal and straw.*

TOP LEFT: *The paint on this door has been scraped and weathered, creating many nuances in the color.*
TOP RIGHT: *The owner, Nicole de Vesian, mixed the paint for the outdoor furniture herself. It mimics the bark of the adjacent trees.*

BOTTOM LEFT: *The layering of color in the house is almost indistinguishable from that in the garden.*
BOTTOM RIGHT: *The silvery blue-green of these plants is a major theme in the design.*

OVERLEAF, LEFT: *The garden is filled with greens that run the gamut from icy frost with hints of blue to warm grasses with gold overtones. The complexity of this color is reflected in the house.*

OVERLEAF, RIGHT: *Artists have long imitated the subtle interactions of warm and cool color in nature. The luminosity of this portrait echoes what is seen in its surroundings.*

ABOVE: *The unadorned, ancient beauty of the facade seemed to command simplicity within.*

OPPOSITE, TOP: *While the rooms have touches of nature, the garden has touches of art. Stone spheres are frequent ornaments.*

OPPOSITE, BOTTOM LEFT: *The circular motif also appears in the* landscaping. *Even the trees and bushes have been cut into spheres.*

OPPOSITE, BOTTOM RIGHT: *Careful arrangements do not eliminate occasional wildness. Hollyhocks are allowed to grow uninhibited in the midst of pavement.*

PAINT MIXING GUIDE

THROUGHOUT THIS BOOK, we've shown rooms whose color, we believe, creates the richest and most complex atmospheres. Whether these spaces are seemingly monochromatic or obviously multi-hued, each room achieves its success through the use of palettes that are balanced across the spectrum. And although the subtleties of each surface cannot be captured exactly in photographs, many of the paints themselves contain a full spectrum of colorants.

What does it mean to create a paint with a full spectrum? Why not just use a commercial brand? If you're looking for a color that has depth, richness, and luminosity—the play or reflection of light through the paint film—you are not likely to find it among the hundreds of samples available at your local dealer. The reason lies in the process of commercial manufacturing: When paint companies create a color, they take short cuts by using few pigments in the simplest combinations. Value and intensity are adjusted with additions of black or white. The dominant color's complement is rarely present. This makes the paint easy to match, but denies it the complexity we see in natural hues.

The pigments that manufacturers use are of two kinds: earth and synthetic. The earth pigments, such as red oxide, burnt umber, yellow oxide, and lamp black, are favored commercially for mixing neutral tones and graying off bright ones. Their opacity results in paint with plenty of covering power but little luminosity. Synthetic pigments like Fast red, Thalo blue, and Hansa yellow are more transparent but have few nuances. They each occupy an extremely narrow range of the spectrum, and they are rarely combined in a way that could give them more breadth. Ironically, these standard synthetics' limited range and high intensity can become assets when these pigments are properly mixed together. When they are combined to create a full spectral range, their bright contrast can give the resulting color dimension and latitude, while their transparency also allows light to circulate. The result is complex color.

Mixing such full-spectrum paints is exacting work. You may not become a color alchemist overnight, but the basic approaches outlined here should enable you to understand what is required to attain richer hues. In the formulas given in this chapter, we have deliberately focused on readily available commercial paint products—all synthetic pigments—whose potential, we believe, has not been exploited.

FORMULATING YOUR OWN COLORS

Mixing your own colors is an illuminating and rewarding process. Careful measurement and record keeping is key. It allows you to see the effect of each drop of pigment added and tells you where to go next. Also, to reproduce the color accurately from one batch to another you need a formula. Paint dealers accomplish this with increment dispensers—the mechanical measuring devices found in every paint store. The most practical home method is to use standard measuring spoons. Here are the guidelines:

MIXING PAINTS AT HOME: THREE NEUTRAL COLORS

	WHITE	LIGHT WARM GRAY	LIGHT BEIGE
Cal-Tint Bulletin Red	¼ teaspoon	1 tablespoon	2 teaspoons
Cal-Tint Orange	¼ teaspoon	2½ teaspoons	2¼ teaspoons
Cal-Tint Interior Yellow	1¼ teaspoons	3 tablespoons & 2 teaspoons	4 tablespoons & 2 teaspoons
Cal-Tint Thalo Green	None	¼ teaspoon	⅛ teaspoon
Cal-Tint Thalo Blue	¼ teaspoon	1 tablespoon	1¼ teaspoons
Cal-Tint Violet	¼ teaspoon	1½ teaspoons	¾ teaspoon

Using standard measuring spoons, add indicated amounts of Cal-Tint Universal Tinting Colorants to one gallon of white tinting base. Cal-Tint is a widely available brand of universal tinting color, and may be used in all standard house paints. Resulting color will vary according to paint brand and finish, i.e., semigloss or flat, oil or latex, etc.

SELECT A MAGAZINE CLIPPING, FABRIC SWATCH, OR PHOTOGRAPH that approximates the color you have in mind. If nothing is available, start with a commercial paint chip as close in color as possible to the color you want. Look at it under the same conditions of light you intend for its use.

OBTAIN THE APPROPRIATE INGREDIENTS. These are tinting bases and universal colorants, all available at paint dealerships or through contractors. The bases

contain varying proportions of white; it is important to choose the base with the amount of white that will make the color as light or as dark as you want it to be. The whitest bases are used to make the lightest colors. (Your paint store or contractor can advise you on this.) Since you need a large volume of base for light colors, it is easiest to formulate these in a minimum of one gallon. Darker colors can be mixed in one-quart batches. At the least, you will need the following universal colorants: Bulletin red, orange, Interior yellow, Thalo green, Thalo blue, and violet.

The pigments selected for teaspoon-measured formulas are Cal-Tint Universal Tinting Colorants, which are widely available in plastic squeeze bottles. They may be added to any brand of paint or type of finish (i.e., oil or latex), but because the bases of different manufacturers vary, our formulas should be used as guides only.

START WITH SMALL AMOUNTS of universal tinting colors. At the very minimum, a successful paint formula should have red, yellow, and blue. Shifting proportions of these three primaries really will get you any color, and in combination they are the shortest route to a full spectrum. The best shades of light and dark green, for example, are mixed from blue and yellow with just a touch of red. A popular color like cream can be made from a white base mixed with small

amounts of red, yellow, and an infinitesimal measure of blue. Red and blue can be combined with the same type of white base to make a violet, which will realize its full potential with just a hint of yellow. In addition to red, yellow, and blue (the primaries), even greater nuance can be achieved by introducing orange, green, and violet (the secondaries).

Cautious experimentation provides the best results, because some colors are more sensitive than others. Yellow, for instance, needs the least of its complement—usually just a minuscule trace of violet—to attain the desired equilibrium. Among synthetic pigments, Thalo green should be used sparingly in creating most light colors, because of its pervasive effect. Our formulas illustrate balances of these elements that may be adjusted to produce countless variations within any given palette.

The earth pigments, although not used in the formulas given in this chapter, play an important role in shades like terra-cotta. Without red oxide and yellow oxide, such colors would look too pink or peach. Earth pigments are also critical to exterior paints because of their resiliency. A good way to give such a paint spectral breadth would be to add synthetic Thalo blue, which also resists fading. If a warm shade needs to be toned down, you could add a drop of blue instead of following standard procedure—adding a drop of black. In fact, avoiding black is one of the most important points in mixing paints. Nature does not cre-

ate grays exclusively from black and white; neither should we. Another neutral, such as plain beige, for instance, is really a combination of red and green that is so well balanced that the color of the paint, when appropriately mixed, appears to be neither ocher nor tan.

TEST YOUR WORK OFTEN. To understand the pigments' interactions, stir in each sequentially. But don't try to attain the perfect formula only by observing the paint in the can; you will see a big difference after it has dried on a surface. (Colors tend to look more yellow when wet, more blue when dry.) As you add each pigment, test the formula on a piece of white cardboard and look at it under the appropriate light. When you think you're close, apply some paint to an area of the wall itself. (For testing, you can dry latex paint quickly with a hair dryer without affecting the color. Oil-based paints will yellow from the heat.)

One of the hardest aspects to gauge when mixing any color is its intensity when applied over a large area. To avoid garish results, the paint in the can may have to appear grayer than you might expect. Once again, testing is the key.

MIXING COLORS WITH YOUR PAINT DEALER

To make a formula that can be reproduced quickly and exactly, you can ask your paint dealer to mix it with an increment dispenser. The recipes that follow—for a light warm gray and a light beige—are both made with this equipment from standard ingredients. The purpose of each is to attain a full spectrum within that color range. Such formulas will have greater proportions of some pigments than others, but none will fail to include the dominant color's complement. (A color's complement can be identified with a standard color wheel available in art supply stores. When experimenting with paint, it is helpful to have one.)

The colorants we have listed here are generic. Every paint store will have the same or comparable ingredients. But because of variations in products from one manufacturer to another, the formulas are approximate.

WORKING WITH A DEALER: TWO NEUTRAL COLORS

	LIGHT WARM GRAY	LIGHT BEIGE
Clear Red (Quinacridone)	6	8
Bright Orange (L.F. Medium)	5	9
Clear Yellow (Hansa)	18	1 ounce 24
Green (Thalo)	½	½
Blue (Thalo)	4	3
Violet (Carbazole)	3	3

With an increment dispenser, add these amounts of universal tinting colorants to one gallon of white tinting base. Colorants listed are generic. Amounts are in 32nds of an ounce. Colors will vary according to paint and colorant brands.

ALTERING COMMERCIAL COLORS

A rich color does not necessarily have to be mixed from scratch. It is always possible to get improved results from one of the commercial formulas just by providing the missing part of the spectrum. Frequently, the amounts of pigment required to enrich standard colors will seem so small as to be almost inconsequential. But never underestimate the effect of a tiny addition. A case in point: A friend was trying to obtain the appropriate shade of beige for her living room walls. When she tried out the paint she had selected on an area of her wall, she found the color to be dull. We learned that the commercial formula contained only red oxide, yellow oxide and black. We asked the dealer to add Thalo blue in the smallest measurable increment—1/64 of an ounce in this case. With this small addition, the color had all the added dimension it needed. Blue, in fact, is the pigment most often missing from the warm neutrals many people choose for their rooms. And it can take literally one drop to achieve the appropriate balance.

Before you can remedy commercial paint, you must look at it in the light of the space at various times of day. When you're certain that you've chosen a color that approximates what you want, test it. You may find that what was a tasteful linen shade of white on a paint chip took on a sallow cast when it was amplified across several feet. And by seeing that a particular white is too yellow, or a pink too powerful, you learn what that particular paint needs: some of the color's complement to temper it and give it a more complex identity. The white that was too yellow can be balanced with blue or violet; the pink can become less strident with the addition of the barest trace of Thalo green.

In practical terms, getting the look you want may mean asking your contractor or paint dealer to go a little beyond the standard procedure. But most are equipped to fulfill such requests.

After experimenting with color, it should be no surprise if the paint you like best is a light, warm neutral. Such formulations account for 90 percent of all colors used in interiors because they are the easiest to live with and allow the greatest variety in their surroundings. Does this mean that after an entire book about color, we're coming back to oyster and sand, buttermilk and cream? Yes, but not the tones you last saw in a schoolroom or a doctor's office. New, richer shades of neutrals can be inspired by a riverbed in France, a weathered shutter in old New Orleans, or a well-worn pair of khaki trousers. They are neutral because they are so very colored. The answer is just that simple. And just that complex.

COLOR NOTEBOOK

RED

Red's nearly palpable power comes from the color's heat. In fact, the warmer the red, the more red it is perceived to be. Shades incorporating orange are more truly red, while bluer tones seem derivative. And the color's most brilliant versions—ruby red, Imari red—appear most substantial. Reds seem not only to advance, but to absorb. They never float; they seem to seep in. Of all colors, red is viewed as most inseparable from its surface.

BLUE

Blue symbolizes both serenity and sadness. Mention blue sky, and images of calm summer afternoons and wide-open spaces come to mind; talk of blue feelings, and the mood can seem as dark as midnight.

The two sides of blue derive from its intrinsic coolness, which can either soothe or chill. Its effect, in architectural spaces as in language, depends on its context. Placed alongside natural wood, blue will heighten the warmth of the material at the same time that it provides a respite from it. But used alone, blue, which appears to recede, can be both visually and psychologically distancing. Its warmer shades, tending toward the green side of the spectrum, are the easiest choices for interiors.

YELLOW

Yellow is a color that doesn't seem to stay put; instead of being at one with a surface, it looks as if it is floating off into the air, pervading the atmosphere like sunshine. As well it should—this hue, falling between the extremes of red and violet, is closest to visible light and is always·perceived as light's natural color. When yellow is placed next to other hues, it appears to be illuminating them much like the sun. And because of its association with light, it creates not only the effect of coming toward the viewer, but of pulling him or her in. It is actually compelling—our eyes are always drawn to a source of light.

GREEN

This hue is unlike anything else in the spectrum—a natural neutral, it incorporates the cool of blue and the heat of yellow. This dual personality enables it to be as effective a backdrop in living spaces as it is in the landscape. Hunter, celadon, and khaki were used in many historic houses as a bridge between nature and architecture. It is the only color that in a dark, intense shade can still be neutral.

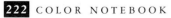

VIOLET

Violet concludes the spectrum and the day. The natural hue toward which all shadows tend, it is by definition a color that is almost absent as soon as it is present—the last echo of visible light.

This ephemeral nature makes violet seem to vanish. If red feels the most tangible of colors, violet feels the least. Rather than appearing integral with a surface, the hue seems to evaporate. This ethereal quality, which makes violet a subtle and valuable ingredient in a color mix, also makes it difficult to use by itself. To gain substance, it should be seen with its complements, whose contrast will give it identity.

INDEX